PMAT

First published in the United States of America in 2009 by

Glitterati Incorporated
225 Central Park West, Suite 305
New York, New York 10024

Telephone 212-362-9119/Fax 646-607-4433
www.GlitteratiIncorporated.com
Email glitterati@verizon.net for inquiries

Photo compositions copyright © Sarah Morgan Karp. Special thanks to the following contributors: Jason Boutsayaphat; Paul Cuoco; Andy Culpin; Justin Haworth; Ned Horton; Cleiton M. Isoton; Hollie Jeans; Lewis Johnston; Adam Lofting; Linda K. Long; LotusHead; Jyn Meyer; Mariusz Swiader; Robert Townsend; Thom Wall; and Timothy Wood.

First edition, 2009

Design and photography: Sarah Morgan Karp/smk-design.com

Library of Congress Cataloging-in-Publication data is available from the publisher.

Hardcover ISBN 13: 978-9793384-5-8

Printed and bound in China by Hong Kong Graphics & Printing Ltd.

9 8 7 6 5 4 3 2 1

PMAT

The Perfect Marriage
Aptitude Test

BY MARY T. CARTY

Glitterati
INCORPORATED

Special thanks goes to Marta Hallett, publisher of Glitterati Incorporated, who believed in the PMAT and made this book a reality; to Signe Bergstrom, whose wise suggestions and editing skills brought the original manuscript to another level; to David Carriere, who gently guided me through the publishing process; to Sarah Morgan Karp, whose design and photos bring added life to the words; and to Julia Cameron, whose book The Artist's Way, taught me to write every day and gave me the encouragement to follow my heart's desire.

Dedication

To Mark Lombard:
My partner, soul mate, writing collaborator,
and best friend. You have loved and
supported me through this roller-coaster
ride called marriage.

CONTENTS

INTRODUCTION

"The secret of a happy marriage remains a secret"

The simple phrase "I do" has the magical power to superglue two people together until death or at least until the divorce proceedings. After joining hands and hearts, the newlyweds retreat down the aisle into a paradoxical world that ranges from nirvana to the black hole. Blinded by romantic love, they enter this new life form called marriage, unaware of the challenges, booby traps, and land mines they will encounter. The wedding reception is followed by the fun-filled honeymoon, which is followed by blissful nest building. In time, however, small irritations begin to mount over the most inane details, like the uncapped toothpaste tube or, worse, your spouse's erratic driving behavior. Then, like a carton of milk that has been left out of the fridge too long, the honeymoon sours and the reality of matrimony sets in. You and your spouse discover the true meaning of the word *wedlock* and wish that you would have:

A. Answered "I don't" at the altar.

B. Listened more carefully to the advice given by bitterly divorced friends or relatives.

C. Majored in marriage at school.

While society provides training programs, degree majors, and a variety of standardized tests, like the Scholastic Aptitude Test (SAT), the Graduate Record Examination (GRE), and the Medical College Admission Test

(MCAT), to prepare people for their career paths, there are no degree programs, internships, or required training for marriage. While there are many resources available to help couples plan their weddings, there is little information on how to prepare for marriage after the honeymoon. Due to this lack of preparation, many couples may feel ill-prepared to handle the stresses and everyday situations marriage can provoke. The *Perfect Marriage Aptitude Test (PMAT)* is offered to prepare and support brides, grooms, and civil-union couples in their quest to build strong, healthy marriages and partnerships.

Marriages are created by the choices couples make on a daily, even minute-to-minute basis, while walking through a variety of situations that can range from a task as simple as divvying up chores to something more complex, like figuring out shared finances. It is the element of choice of actions, thoughts, attitudes, and responses that determines the structure and quality of a marriage.

The *PMAT* focuses on the response-ability of partners in everyday situations. There are 200 possible marriage situations offered, with 600 multiple-choice responses that help each partner assess his or her response style, hints on how to improve basic communication skills, and suggestions on how to take care of your marriage and yourself.

Chapter 1, "Building a Marriage One Decision at a Time," includes a short definition of marriage that is the premise of the *PMAT*, a brief overview of the concept of "partnership power," and directions for the multiple-choice assessment test. Chapters 2 through 9 organize the multiple-choice *PMAT* test into easily digestible sections, with each chapter focusing on specific marital issues; chapter 10, "Response-ability," includes information relating to the test results and the assessment process; chapter 11, "Let's Talk," provides tools for clear and honest communication; chapter 12, "Taking Care of the Self" contains helpful reminders and tips on the importance of investing time for self-care, which benefits both you and your partner; chapter 13, "A Parting Gift," contains simple suggestions that can enhance any marriage.

More than a book, the *PMAT* is a communication tool kit that can be used throughout your marriage. Use it to chart your growth by comparing your notes, thoughts, and answers with your partner's so that you both will be better equipped to deal with the issues that may visit (and potentially revisit) your marriage.

It is my hope that the information presented here might be helpful to those couples thinking about getting married and those who have already crossed the wedding threshold. While it may take a short amount of time to take the *PMAT* test, its lasting effects should be felt long after the exchange of vows and for many years still to come.

Get ready, get set, and turn the page to begin.

—MARY T. CARTY

CHAPTER ONE:

BUILDING A MARRIAGE ONE DECISION AT A TIME

"Marriage ain't easy, but it's great most of the time."

—SEAN PENN

Marriage can be the most beautiful and intimate relationship two people can share. Though the divorce rate has increased, there are still couples all over the world who choose to invest in and celebrate their special love by getting married. In marriage, they can support each other, work to make the relationship stronger, and achieve goals and dreams to form a unique partnership; this "partnership power" can enable them to have a richer life together than living alone.

Working together to attain goals in a marriage and supporting the life direction and gifts of each partner creates a support system that fosters growth of the individual and of the marriage. Combining each individual's skills, likes, dislikes, and dreams into an efficient team built on one vision takes time, and is an ongoing process.

The wedding vows mark the beginning of the process. Reflecting a couple's willingness to cooperate with each other and their desire to love and support one another through all of life's ups and downs, these vows express a commitment to each other to create the kind of marriage and relationship both parties desire. It's only later, after the wedding, that the vows get put to the test.

Within a marriage, there are large issues, like those surrounding intimacy and financial planning, that need to be addressed along with more practical concerns, like deciding what time the alarm clock needs to be set in the morning and figuring out what to do on the weekends. If couples have lived together before marriage, they have already done some of this work, but they may face new challenges related to more complicated issues. For couples who are living together for the first time, each day presents challenges that affect both individuals.

The premise of the *PMAT* is that people create the marriage they will have by these everyday choices and countless decisions they make relating to family, household, job, money, and health issues. Both newlyweds and long-time married couples face an immediate challenge: to develop the proper skills to cope with sharing these life decisions while retaining their own sense of identity and, at the same time, showing respect for the other person, the love of their life. Two of the most important skills in marriage are the ability to make sound decisions and the ability to communicate with clarity, empathy, and respect. The *PMAT* offers couples a chance to practice each of these skills.

TESTING, TESTING, 1,2,3

The 200 multiple-choice questions that begin the next chapter present you and your partner with situations and options that may be unfamiliar and/or unexpected. There are three options presented for every question. These options or answers give you a general idea of your typical response style. "Response style" refers to how you react to a situation via words, actions, or inactions. The response styles are divided into the following four categories:

ULTIMATE RESPONSE STYLE includes a willingness to collaborate, cooperate, and compromise, as well as invest time and energy in taking positive actions that enhance the marriage.

COMPETENT RESPONSE STYLE includes a willingness to discuss issues and be open to the spirit of cooperation.

INCONSISTENT RESPONSE STYLE includes a tendency to sometimes be open, affectionate, talkative, respectful, and present, yet at other times to show disrespect, refuse to discuss issues, and/or choose to isolate.

CLUELESS RESPONSE STYLE includes a tendency to criticize, to show disrespect, and a refusal to collaborate or cooperate.

The directions for taking the *PMAT* are simple: Take time to read each question and visualize the situation. Then read and visualize each of the options and choose whichever you think is the best answer by filling in the response sheet provided in the back of the book. If you have a better option than those presented, use the blank space (option D) to write in your own. Please note, however, that in order to get an accurate response-assessment score, the answers must be A, B, or C. There is no time limit in taking this test. Instead of rushing through it in one sitting, take the time to do one section at a time. When the option sheet is complete, turn to chapter 10 for the response-assessment descriptions and scoring directions.

This test is not scientifically based; it is intended to give readers a lighthearted look at examples of possible marriage situations with a variety of responses. Couples are given an opportunity to discuss how they might deal with a number of issues that may or may not occur in their marriage.

A Meditation for Preparation

BEFORE YOU BEGIN THE TEST,
review the following list of statements:

No two people are exactly alike.

No two people think exactly alike.

You cannot read your partner's mind.

Your partner cannot read your mind.

We are human and make mistakes.

It is impossible to change other people.

It is possible to change your actions
and attitudes.

Treat the other person the same way
you would like to be treated.

People have different opinions, likes,
dislikes, and beliefs.

It is a human quality to have and
show emotions.

It is a human quality for your partner to
have and to show emotions.

It takes courage to accept differences.

It takes courage to forgive.

Patience is a virtue.

No one is perfect.

Love conquers fear.

Chapter Two:
Home and Harmony

Couples usually share the majority of their "together time" and space in the home, making it the backdrop to an endless series of challenging situations. The following examples cover a range of topics that include chores, decorating, climate preferences, and how to navigate shared space. Before proceeding any further, keep in mind that these situations may or may not occur in your marriage. They are presented as a way for you to envision what your response may be to a given situation. Remember: No two people have the exact same thoughts, behaviors, expectations, opinions, talents, gifts, or skills, and each individual has been brought up in different circumstances, which have influenced their thoughts and behaviors.

1. YOUR PARTNER FREQUENTLY SQUISHES UP THE tube of toothpaste, while you prefer to roll it up neatly. One morning, you find the tube of toothpaste squished up, its cap off, and a glob of dried toothpaste clogging its opening. You:

A. Clean up the mess, roll up the tube, and put on the cap. (Note: If this situation occurs more than ten times, consider buying your own tube.)

B. Lose control, get upset, and scream like a banshee.

C. Discuss your preferences and ask that the cap be replaced.

D. _____

2. IT IS 98 DEGREES OUTSIDE AND THE AIR CONDItioner is set to a zone that requires thermal underwear and flannel attire. Your partner likes to keep cool, and you like to feel comfortable, but at a decidedly warmer temperature. You:

A. Let your partner know the level of your discomfort and ask for a compromise.

B. Continue "the battle of the thermostat" on a daily basis.

C. Find another living space with temperatures to your liking.

D. _____

3. **YOU LEFT YOUR WINTER BOOTS NEAR THE DOOR** to avoid tracking dirt into the house/apartment. You were remiss and did not put them away. You look for them the next day, but they have vanished. You finally find them on the back porch in a frozen state, causing much discomfort when you put them on to go to work. When you ask your partner about the boots not being where you left them, you are told they were moved for you. You:

A. Widen your eyes, wave your arms, and yell, "Keep your hands off my belongings!" and then hide something of your partner's.

B. Say, "Thank you."

C. Kindly let your partner know that you are an adult and are capable of taking care of your own belongings.

D. _____

4. **WHILE CUTTING THE GRASS, YOUR PARTNER** mows over your prized iris bed. You:

A. Say nothing, but put up a fence to protect the area.

B. Explain that you are upset and suggest that he/she buy and plant a few flowering plants.

C. Are so angry you say nothing and the next time he/she asks for a haircut, you trim short . . . really short.

D. _____

5. THERE ARE DARK STREAKS ON THE KITCHEN
floor from your partner's shoes . . . again. After addressing this issue
about 100 times before by requesting that either the shoes be removed or
the floor cleaned, you:

A. Calmly let your expectations be known for the 101st time, asking
your partner to clean the floor.

B. Clean the floor and harbor anger for hours.

C. Call for a brainstorming meeting to discuss household matters and
suggest that you and your partner hire a cleaning person.

D. _____ _____

6. THE DISHES NEED TO BE DONE. YOU ALWAYS DO
the dishes and are sick of it. You:

A. Go on strike and wait until your partner does the dishes or brings up
the issue.

B. Voice your concern and ask about sharing the responsibility.

C. Start using paper plates and plasticware.

D. _____ _____

7. YOU'VE RETURNED FROM A WALK IN 90-DEGREE
heat and are dehydrated. You have visualized a tall, ice-cold glass of
juice, and can almost hear the clink of the ice cubes on the side of the
glass. Yet, you discover that the ice-cube tray is empty. When you reach
for the other tray, you find that it is empty as well. You:

A. Leave the trays out unfilled and ask that they be refilled, while you
wonder how your partner was able to graduate from high school without
enough common sense to refill ice-cube trays.

B. Suggest buying a new refrigerator that makes ice automatically.

C. Fill the trays this time and request that your partner is responsible for
filling the ice trays that he/she emptied.

D. _____ _____

8. AFTER A BUSY DAY, YOU LOOK FORWARD TO SET-tling into your favorite chair and reading a best-selling novel. You flip the switch on the lamp and nothing happens. Your partner says, "Oh, yeah, that went out last week." You go to the closet to look for a lightbulb. The package is empty because your partner used the last lightbulb and did not replace the supply or put them on the shopping list. You:

A. Give your partner a lecture on the responsibility of replacing lightbulbs and other household articles.

B. Decide that the next time you're out shopping, you will stock up on lightbulbs.

C. Bring up the issue the next time you both sit down to have a discussion about household issues.

D. _____

9. YOU ARE PUTTING YOUR CLOTHES AWAY AND cannot finish because your partner has once again "borrowed" hangers from your closet. You:

A. State that you feel that your space and belongings have been violated.

B. Realize that hangers are cheap and buy extras for both of you.

C. Go into your partner's closet, reclaim your hangers, and leave your partner's clothes on the floor.

D. _____

10. YOU WAKE UP IN THE MIDDLE OF THE NIGHT AND feel a chill. You get out of bed to check the thermostat, only to discover that the furnace isn't working. You wake your partner to help you figure out the problem and discover that the fuel tank is empty. You:

A. Yell and scream because the feeling of cold ranks up there with excruciating pain.

B. Blame your partner for not taking the needed precautions to handle this important household responsibility.

C. Suggest ordering automatic fuel service and discuss who will make the phone call to have some fuel delivered immediately.

D. _____

11. THE SINK LEAKS. YOU BRING UP THE ISSUE, AND your partner replies that he/she will attend to it. Days pass and the drip-drip-drip continues. You ask again. Your partner reacts with anger, saying that it will get done when there is time. Another week goes by and the dripping continues. You:

A. Thank your partner for offering to attend to it and note that you've called a plumber because you understand that your partner has been very busy.

B. Say nothing and call a plumber.

C. Keep waiting, nagging, and hoping that the promise of correcting the dripping will be fulfilled.

D. _____

12. THE VACUUM CLEANER DOES NOT FUNCTION well. When it does start, the sound is loud and annoying to you, but not to your partner. You:

A. Raise the issue, present the facts, and ask what your partner thinks should be done.

B. Go to the store, pull out the credit card, and buy a shiny, new vacuum cleaner.

C. State that you intend to go on strike and will no longer vacuum the house without a new or repaired vacuum cleaner.

D. _____

13. YOU'VE ALREADY GONE THOUGH THE DECISION-
making process about who does the laundry. One important issue that
was not discussed, however, was where the dirty laundry should be
stored. Your partner has chosen more often than not to leave clothes on
the bedroom floor and other places. You:

A. Pick your partner's dirty clothes up and put them in the hamper.

B. Pick your partner's dirty clothes up and do his/her laundry as well as
yours, without mentioning anything.

C. Leave the clothes where they are and clearly request that the clothes
not be left on the floor in the future.

D. _____

14. YOUR PARTNER NEVER HAD TO DO LAUNDRY
while growing up and never learned how to operate a washing
machine. You:

A. Offer to give your partner a crash course on detergents, the loading
process, and the spin cycle.

B. Do the laundry for both of you without discussion.

C. Volunteer to take care of your partner's laundry in exchange for him/
her to take care of one of your chores.

D. _____

15. YOUR LIFE PARTNER HAS A BEAUTIFUL HEAD OF
hair. However, as you prepare to take a shower, you spot a really gross
hairball in the drain. You:

A. Ask your partner in a kind, gentle manner to remove it.

B. Leave a laminated note for your partner on the water handle, telling
him/her to clean the drain.

C. Claim another bathroom, if you have one, as your own.

D. _____

16. YOUR PARTNER SURPRISES YOU BY CLEANING
and reorganizing the workbench/worktable. You were in the middle of a project and now have to begin again. You:

A. Tell your partner that you were in the middle of a project and now you are faced with taking the time to start over again, and request that next time he/she ask first before reorganizing a work area.

B. Get upset, but recognize your partner was trying to help and say, "Thank you."

C. Reorganize the area and resent your partner's "help."

D. _____

17. YOU JUST MOVED IN TO YOUR NEW HOME/
apartment. You believe that taking off your shoes protects the rugs and floor, and saves vacuuming time. It is automatic for you to remove your shoes. The thought doesn't cross your partner's mind. You:

A. Patronize your partner, asking as you would a child, "Did you take your shoes off?"

B. Don't allow your partner in the house with shoes on.

C. Remind your partner that you requested that his/her shoes be taken off and request that he/she share the responsibility of cleaning the rugs and the floors.

D. _____

18. MONTHS HAVE GONE BY AFTER THE WEDDING,
maybe even years. You wake up one day, glance at the bathroom, and realize that you have always cleaned the shower/bathtub. Your partner never has, and you are sick and tired of doing it. You:

A. Tell your partner that after cleaning the shower/bathtub all of this time, you have decided to pass on that chore to him/her.

B. Say nothing, continue to do the task, and play the role of martyr.

C. Ask for help and a meeting to discuss the possibility of trading chores or hiring someone to help with the housework.

D. _____

19. YOUR PARTNER GETS UP EARLIER THAN YOU
and makes his/her side of the bed while you are still in it. Somehow this doesn't seem normal, maybe a bit obsessive-compulsive. You:

A. Appreciate the making of his/her side of the bed, considering that some partners never make even half the bed.

B. Ask for an explanation and give thanks that your partner doesn't make the whole bed while you are still in it.

C. Tell people about your partner's quirky behavior, just for laughs.

D. _____

20. YOU NOTICED DURING COURTING THAT YOUR
partner had the habit of leaving bath towels on the floor. That was no problem then because you were in the head-over-heels state of love. During the honeymoon, the chambermaid took care of the wet towels on the floor. The honeymoon is over and your partner still leaves the towels on the floor. You:

A. Give the parental act-like-a-responsible-adult lecture on how wet towels do not belong on the floor.

B. Kindly request that the towels be picked up.

C. Say nothing, leave the towels on the floor, and hope your partner's behavior will change.

D. _____

21. YOU COME HOME FROM A HARD DAY OF WORK
and your partner has rearranged the living room for the nth time. You
don't like change and want the room to stay the same. You:

A. Jump down your partner's throat and state that he/she has no right to
keep moving furniture around.

B. Ask to have a discussion about changing the floor plan and communicate that you have a right to share in decision making about decorating.

C. Ask your partner if there are any unresolved issues that need to be
dealt with, because you once read that shifting furniture around can be a
symptom of unresolved conflicts or a sign of desire for a life change.

D. _____

22. YOUR PARTNER DROPS SOMETHING ON THE
floor, bends down to pick it up, and exclaims in horror how filthy the
area is under the refrigerator. You:

A. Feel guilty, apologize, and take care of it right away.

B. Thank your partner for pointing it out and note that you both should
sit down to talk about all of the areas in the house that need attention
and decide how to split up those chores.

C. Hand your partner the mop and state that if it is bothering him/her
that much he/she can clean it immediately.

D. _____

23. EACH SPRING, YOU HAVE AN INSTINCT TO DO
annual spring-cleaning. However, your partner, born without that particular instinct, hoards everything, saving all clothes, shoes, string, a broken
lamp, etc. The stuff fills drawers, the garage, and closets. You can't stand
it any longer. You:

A. Go ahead and throw stuff way, not telling your partner, thinking that
it will never be missed.

B. Set up a meeting to discuss your need for a neater home.

c. Accept this idiosyncrasy and designate a room/area that is dedicated to your "partner's stuff."

D. _____

24. YOU HAVE A HEADACHE AND GO TO THE MEDI-
cine cabinet for aspirin but find none. You are in pain and upset that your partner evidently depleted the aspirin supply without refilling it. You:

A. Tear into your partner for using all of the aspirin and not replenishing the supply.

B. Say nothing, buy your own bottle, and hide it.

c. Ask your partner where the aspirin might be. If the reply is that there is none, ask that the supply be replenished.

D. _____

25. AS YOU SETTLE YOUR BELONGINGS IN A NEW
home, the time comes to unpack books into the bookcase. You realize there is one bookcase in the living room and you both have a lot of books. You discuss the situation with your partner and you agree to equally divide the space. The job is complete and your partner criticizes the appearance of your books' arrangement and seems a bit queasy about your choice of reading materials. You:

A. Take your books out and let your partner have the whole bookcase so you won't have to hear him/her complain about it anymore.

B. Tell your partner that your books are a reflection of your personality and likes, and ask that your arrangement and selection be accepted.

c. Diagnose your partner as being overly critical and suggest that he/she loosen up.

D. _____

26. THE HOLIDAYS ARE OVER AND THE PHOTOS ARE back from the processor. You and your partner enjoy looking at them. The photos sit on the dining-room table for weeks. After suggesting that they be put in an album with the rest of the photos, you:

A. Ask to share this task.

B. Start getting them in order, spending your free time to date and sort them.

C. Throw them in a box in the hope that they will organize themselves.

D. _____

27. YOU'VE JUST ANSWERED NATURE'S CALL. YOU reach for the toilet paper and discover your partner used the last of the roll and did not put a new roll on the hanger. This has occurred more than once. The fact of the matter is that he/she has never replaced a roll. You:

A. Lead your partner into the bathroom and give him/her a lesson on the hows and whys of replacing toilet paper, as you would a child.

B. Place an extra roll an arm's length away.

C. Mention this issue the next time household issues are discussed.

D. _____

28. YOUR PARTNER WASHED THE CLOTHES, AND there is white lint on all of the dark clothes because the pockets weren't emptied of paper tissues. You:

A. Rant and rave and accuse him/her of ruining your clothes.

B. Throw the clothes back in the dryer to remove the lint. Thank your partner for doing the laundry and suggest he/she check the pockets beforehand.

C. Give a parental-style lecture on the proper way to do laundry.

D. _____

29. YOU WERE BROUGHT UP TO PICK UP DISHES

after yourself. Your partner wasn't taught this habit. Soon after you return from the honeymoon, you notice dirty dishes all over the house. You:

A. Want to make your partner love you so you pick them up, playing the part of parent or maid.

B. Clearly state your request that dishes not be left all over the house.

C. Leave a note near the dishes reminding your partner to clean up after him/herself.

D. _____

CHAPTER THREE:
FOOD, FITNESS, AND HEALTH

"Some people ask the secret of our long marriage.
We take time to go to a restaurant two times
a week. A little candlelight, dinner, soft music
and dancing. She goes Tuesdays, I go Fridays."

—HENRY "HENNY" YOUNGMAN

Food issues, such as diet restrictions and budget constraints, present a variety of challenges for marriage partners. Since food plays such a large role in a couple's life, the following questions could be addressed: "Who is doing the grocery shopping and who is doing the cooking?" "Who is planning the menu and what time will meals be shared?" "How will diet restrictions be addressed and will this responsibility be shared by both people?"

Closely related to food issues are health and fitness. Getting regular exercise, as well as eating a healthy diet can contribute to overall fitness and may guard against disease. Marriage vows often include the phrase "in sickness and in health, until death do us part," implying that couples may well consider taking steps to stay healthy for the sake of their marriage, themselves, and their family.

The following situations and options relate to food, fitness, and health:

I. YOUR PARTNER SUGGESTS GOING OUT TO EAT

and asks you to choose the restaurant. You suggest your favorite restaurant and he/she says, "I'm not in the mood for that. Why don't you make another choice?" You make another choice that is voted down. You:

A. Identify this behavior as some kind of control game.

B. Keep making suggestions and hope to reach an agreement.

C. Reply that you have made your last suggestion and that the decision is now up to him/her.

D. _____

2. YOU DON'T LIKE TO COOK. YET, DURING THE

first year of marriage, your partner gives you a new, souped-up blender for your birthday. You:

A. Are disappointed at the lack of sensitivity and creativity, but graciously accept the gift and mention that you enjoy personal gifts.

B. Lie through your teeth and pretend to love the gift, yet wonder how your partner could be so oblivious to your likes and dislikes.

C. Say, "Won't it be fun for both of us to learn how to use it?"

D. _____

3. YOU BOTH ENJOY GOING OUT TO EAT. WHO

doesn't? You are at a new place on the waterfront and the waiter leads you to a table overlooking a fabulous water view. Your partner immediately takes the seat with the better view. A red flag goes up. Your partner always seems to take the seat with a view, leaving you to stare at the wall. You:

A. Make a miniscene by pouting and accusing your partner of taking the best seat. Your tantrum puts a damper on the evening and gives the other diners something to talk about.

B. Realize that you would like to have the nice view, ask to change seats, and suggest taking turns in the future.

C. Choose to be a pushover and say nothing.

D. _____

4. YOUR DOCTOR HAS SUGGESTED THAT YOU EAT A healthier diet and get regular exercise because your cholesterol level is high. You:

A. Tell your partner that you are concerned about the results of the test and ask for help to modify your diet and support to follow an exercise program.

B. Choose not to make any changes and neglect telling your partner about the test results.

C. Demand that your partner follow the same exercise and diet guidelines that your doctor has suggested for you.

D. _____

5. ONE OF THE WEDDING PRESENTS YOU RECEIVED was a shiny new toaster oven. You try it out, and the toast burns because your partner set the oven on high, the way he/she likes it. You:

A. Demand that the setting be set back to your liking.

B. Remind yourself that each person has a preference and that it is very simple to readjust the dial.

C. Complain about it daily.

D. _____

6. YOU HATE TO CLEAN THE REFRIGERATOR, BUT DO it regularly. Your partner doesn't clean the refrigerator. Then one day, he/she makes a big production out of some mold on leftovers and says, "I can't believe you let this happen!" You:

A. Get upset because you've quietly cleaned the refrigerator in the past and have never once gotten a thank-you.

B. State appreciation for the observation and suggest he/she take over the job of regularly cleaning the refrigerator.

C. Suggest sharing the responsibility because you have been extra busy and have not had the time to take care of all the chores.

D. _____

7. YOU WENT OUT OF YOUR WAY TO MAKE A NICE
dinner and tried a new fish recipe. You were criticized for the entire meal because of a chance appearance of a bone in the fish. You:

A. Announce that the chore of cooking will now be shared more often.

B. Cry and agree that you are a terrible cook.

C. Don't take it personally. Some things are out of your control—like a bone in fish and criticism from other people.

D. _____

8. YOU RELISH YOUR MORNING JUMP-START CUP OF
java. You get the coffee machine going and are ready to savor the first sip. You pour the coffee into your favorite cup, add sugar, open the refrigerator, and reach for the milk. Much to your dismay, there is no milk or cream. You:

A. Turn from Dr. Jekyll to Mrs./Mr. Hyde, have a tantrum, and verbally attack your partner.

B. Remind yourself it is not the end of the world and get a cup on the way to work.

C. Ask your partner to pick up some milk on the way home from work, since he/she drank the last of it.

D. _____

9. You like your coffee weak. Your partner
likes it strong. You:

A. Complain each morning that your partner fixes the coffee too strong and this creates a daily ongoing conflict.

B. Make your own pot of coffee.

C. Add a bit of water to dilute the strong coffee.

D. _____

10. Your partner does not believe in owning
a saltshaker or using salt in cooking, saying that food is naturally salty. You, on the other hand, love salt. You:

A. State that you have the right to use as much salt as you want without being criticized.

B. Use salt in moderation when cooking, out of respect for your partner's taste buds.

C. Complain that his/her cooking lacks any flavor.

D. _____

11. You hear the "ready" bell on the microwave
stove. The repeated beep is annoying and continues because your partner did not reset the timer. You:

A. Turn the timer off. Again.

B. Nag your partner, saying, "Haven't I told you a hundred times to reset the timer?"

C. Leave a reminder note next to the microwave.

D. _____

12. Your partner has accepted the responsi-
bility of shopping for groceries. There is hardly any food in the house and you are hungry. You:

A. Assume that your partner doesn't love you anymore, is shirking his/her responsibility, and has concocted a brilliant, subtle plan to starve you to death.

B. Ask if there is a meal planned and offer to help.

C. Head out to the store to do some grocery shopping.

D. _____

13. YOU HAVE READ THAT REFINED WHITE FLOUR products are not very nutritional. You decide to only buy multigrain bread. Your partner demands that you cook and serve the food he/she was served growing up, which includes plain, white bread. You:

A. Comply.

B. Apologize for not discussing the issue and remind him/her that he/she is free to prepare his/her own food.

C. State that you are making a change in diet for health reasons and provide an open invitation to share this new food concept.

D. _____

14. YOUR PARTNER HAS DECIDED TO RUN A MARATHON. Rather then run a half hour a few times a week, his/her running lasts for hours, even on weekends. Additionally, the marathon has become the main topic of conversation with you and everyone else. The amount of time spent running outweighs your time together and interferes with meals and weekend plans. You:

A. Draw a pie chart to demonstrate how this activity is disrupting your marriage.

B. Adopt the philosophy "if you can't beat them, join them." You drag out your running shoes and start a running program. Not only do you share something else in common with your partner, you get some exercise, too.

c. Remember that it is important to support your partner, and accept the fact that he/she may not be available to spend more time together until after the marathon.

D. _____

15. WHEN YOU AND YOUR PARTNER GOT MARRIED, you both smoked. Since then, you've stopped and your partner has continued. You are concerned about his/her health and do not want the scent of cigarette smoke in the house. You:

A. Suggest that a smoking zone be created outside.

B. Suggest that he/she try to quit.

c. Leave graphic photos of cancerous lungs around the house.

D. _____

16. YOU NOTICE YOUR PARTNER'S ALCOHOL CON-sumption is higher than usual. You:

A. State your concern because you are aware that the need to drink on a daily basis may be a sign of a problem.

B. Join in the party mode.

c. Suggest that counseling may be an important first step to deal with the issue.

D. _____

17. YOU AWAKE WITH SERIOUS FLU SYMPTOMS ON A workday. You:

A. Remind yourself that your workplace provides sick days and make the decision to stay home, rest, and take care of your health.

B. Force yourself to go to work, even though you know you will not be very productive.

c. Complain to your partner.

D. _____

18. YOUR PARTNER COMPLAINS OF STOMACH PROB-
lems and how these problems have had a negative effect on his/her
appetite. You:

A. Listen and ask if there is anything you can do to help.

B. Suggest that your partner see a doctor.

c. Wish that your partner would just stop complaining.

D. _____

19. YOU NOTICE THAT YOU HAVE GAINED ENOUGH
weight that you need to buy new clothes. You:

A. Ask your partner to help you change your diet and start an
exercise regimen because you want to lose some weight.

B. Blame your partner's cooking for your weight gain.

c. Buy a few new outfits and hope that the weight will
magically disappear.

D. _____

20. YOU NOTICE THAT YOUR PARTNER IS GAINING
weight and not exercising. You:

A. Lecture him/her on the importance of healthy eating habits
and exercise.

B. Tell him/her that you are no longer attracted to him/her.

c. Ask him/her if there is anything that you can do to help him/her
get into better physical shape.

D. _____

21. YOUR PARTNER EXERCISES HOURS AND HOURS on end. You are concerned about his/her obsessive focus on exercise, his/her dramatic weight loss, and the fact that little time is spent on any other activities. You:

A. Leave magazine articles around the house concerning fitness addiction and the dangers of overexercising.

B. State your concerns.

C. Ask if your partner is aware of the excessive time element and the weight loss.

D. _____

22. YOU READ THAT WALKING IS A GREAT OVERALL exercise, and you think it is a good idea for you and your partner to take frequent walks. You:

A. Invite him/her to walk with you.

B. Expect him/her to match your enthusiasm and volunteer to walk with you.

C. Tell your partner he/she is out of shape and needs to start walking to get fit.

D. _____

23. YOUR PARTNER HAS BEEN DIAGNOSED WITH diabetes. You:

A. State your concern and ask what you can do to help.

B. Continue to bake desserts, because desserts are a part of your regular meal habit, and you refuse to change your eating patterns.

C. Worry morning, evening, and night that your partner will get very sick with the disease, and you wonder what will happen to you then?

D. _____

24. YOUR SPOUSE HAS BEEN COMPLAINING OF
physical problems, and the doctor has ordered an invasive X-ray exam. You are tired of listening to your partner's fear and anxiety surrounding this test. You:

A. Tell your partner that you are tired of listening to him/her and ask that he/she change the subject.

B. Suggest doing something you both enjoy as a way to take his/her mind off the upcoming exam.

C. Continue to listen to your partner's concerns and offer to accompany your partner to the appointment.

D. _____ _____

25. THERE IS A DEATH IN YOUR PARTNER'S FAMILY.
You go to the funeral, and your partner shows no sign of grief. You wonder if this is normal. You:

A. Buy a book on grief, read it, and give it to your partner as a way to help him/her better cope.

B. Conclude that your partner has no feelings and wonder if his/her reaction would be the same if the loss were of you.

C. Extend your love, give lots of hugs, and reassure your partner that you are available if he/she wants to talk or cry.

D. _____

26. YOU FIND YOURSELF BEHAVING MORE AND
more like your mother/father, and not necessarily in a good way. You desperately want to change this behavioral pattern. You:

A. Go to therapy for professional help.

B. Ask your partner to help you identify and change this behavior.

C. Accept the concept that there is nothing you can do to change.

D. _____

27. YOUR PARTNER PLANNED ON BECOMING A CPA,
but after getting a degree in accounting he/she flunked the CPA exam and has taken it hard. In fact, your partner appears not to be interested in much and seems depressed. You:

A. Share your observation, and suggest that he/she see a counselor/therapist.

B. Tell your partner to get over it and just lighten up.

C. Ask your partner if he/she would like to talk about it or would like some suggestions on how to prepare for the next exam.

D. _____

28. A PROJECT AT WORK IS CAUSING YOUR PARTNER
so much stress that he/she comes home exhausted and obsesses on the issue throughout dinner and well into the night. You:

A. Say nothing, figuring that he/she will eventually get over it by morning, even though he/she tosses and turns all night.

B. Offer to do something to help him/her relax, like giving him/her a massage.

C. Give your partner moral support and offer to talk through ideas and act as a sounding board for him/her.

D. _____

29. YOUR PARTNER IS SO STRESSED-OUT ABOUT A
possible promotion, he/she may appear to be listening to you, but instead, his/her mind is somewhere else. It is impossible to have a relationship in this mode. You:

A. State your concern and announce that you are choosing to do another activity because you feel like you are being ignored.

B. Give a lecture on the importance of listening and the rudeness of not genuinely listening.

c. Give verbal and emotional support by letting your partner know that you understand that this is a difficult time and wish him/her the best.

D. _____

30. YOUR PARTNER SEEMS TO SLEEP QUITE A BIT
and doesn't seem interested in doing many activities. You are worried because he/she appears depressed. You:

A. State your concern and ask if he/she would like to talk about it.

B. Suggest getting professional help.

c. Worry morning, noon, and night, and hope that the problem goes away on its own.

D. _____

31. SOME ISSUES FROM THE PAST HAVE CREPT UP,
and you decide that you need to seek some professional help. Your partner says that the idea is ridiculous because there is nothing wrong with you. You:

A. Go ahead with your plan anyway.

B. Explain to your partner that you really do need some help getting over a bad experience from the past, and ask for his/her support

c. Agree with your partner, do nothing, and continue to feel inner angst.

D. _____

CHAPTER FOUR:

TOGETHERNESS

"Love and marriage, love and marriage, go together like a horse and carriage…"

—SAMMY CAHN

There will be good times. There will be difficult times. There will be busy times, as well as leisurely times. The quality of time spent together sets a tone for the marriage. From vacations to quiet nights at home watching a movie, couples are challenged to decide how to invest their energy and spend their time, sometimes together and sometimes apart. The challenge is to balance work, marriage, personal responsibilities, and goals.

Each person has their own ideas, opinions, likes and dislikes concerning what to do with their time. The key is to share activities that bring both partners joy and to show support to the other in times of need. The following scenarios look at leisure time and vacations, travel, and events with family, friends, and acquaintances:

1. AFTER A LONG WINTER, SPRING HAS SPRUNG, AND you and your partner are on the first road trip of the season. You open your car window to enjoy the fresh air. Your partner rolls up the automatic windows and turns on the air conditioner. You:

A. Say that you prefer the windows down and ask that your opinion be considered when decisions are made that affect you.

B. Put up with the inconvenience and act like a martyr.

C. Take your own car the next time.

D. _____

2. YOUR PARTNER BORROWS YOUR CAR TO DO SOME errands. The next day you are on your way to work and the car engine starts to act funny. You soon find your car out of gas on a four-lane highway. You are going to be late for work. After using your cell phone to call a service station for help, you:

A. Pound the steering wheel, cuss your partner, and vow to never lend your car again.

B. Call your partner to note your frustration and ask for an explanation.

C. Stay angry with your partner for not filling the tank.

D. _____

3. YOUR PARTNER SUGGESTS A FRIENDLY GAME OF cards. You agree and enjoy the game until you begin to lose. You notice that you are no longer having fun and hate to lose. You:

A. Say nothing, put on a sour face, and never play cards with your partner again.

B. Let go of the anger, then let your partner know that you need to learn not to take a card game so seriously.

C. Challenge him/her to another game and change your attitude.

D. _____

4. YOUR PARTNER ALWAYS DRIVES THE CAR WHEN you both go out. You question this behavior as being a control issue. You suggested that you drive on this trip, and your suggestion was ignored. You:

A. Get angry and cop a resentment.

B. State that you also like to drive and would like the opportunity to do so.

C. Sit back and enjoy the ride.

D. _____

5. YOUR PARTNER HAS AGREED TO "LET" YOU DRIVE the car, and you thank him/her for obliging your request. You back out of the driveway, and the following comments are made during a five-mile journey: "Did you see that car?" "If you hurry, you can make the light." "If you go the back way we'll save time." You:

A. Respond by saying, "If you'd get off my back, I'd appreciate it."

B. Go under the speed limit and take the really long way.

C. Ask politely that there be no criticism.

D. _____

6. WHILE YOUR PARTNER IS DRIVING ON A BUSY highway, you notice the gas tank is almost empty. You see a gas station and suggest stopping. Instead, your partner proceeds past the gas station. Ten minutes down the road, the motor sputters as the car runs out of gas. You:

A. Immediately get into the I-told-you-so mode and remain bitter for the rest of the day.

B. Call your partner immature for wanting to live on the edge and threaten to take the family car away until he/she learns how to be more responsible.

C. Remember that you too have run out of gas, cut him/her some slack, and refuse to let the incident affect your day.

D. _____

7. WHILE DRIVING TO AN EVENT IN A NEW AREA,
you both find yourselves lost and late. The map and directions do not
seem to be helpful. You are unsure where to turn next, and your partner
just keeps driving. You:

A. Sit and quietly let your anger and frustration increase.

B. Suggest stopping or calling for directions.

C. Give the why-do-you-continue-to-drive-when-we-are-lost lecture.

D. _____

8. YOU ARE RIDING WITH YOUR PARTNER, WHO IS
usually a responsible, mature adult. As the car becomes part of a traffic
jam, your partner regresses to acting like a child. You:

A. Say that you understand that this is a frustrating situation. Then
add that a change in attitude doesn't cost a penny.

B. Keep in mind that your partner's attitude and actions are beyond
your control.

C. Criticize him/her for acting like a spoiled brat.

D. _____

9. A PERSON ERRATICALLY PULLS IN FRONT OF THE
car, causing a dangerous situation. Your partner calls the person an idiot
and flips the person the bird. You:

A. Remind him/her that this sort of action may provoke an even more
aggressive, dangerous response.

B. Give a parental-type lesson on road etiquette.

C. Continue to read your book and totally ignore his/her
infantile behavior.

D. _____

10. THE HONEYMOON ISN'T EVEN OVER, AND YOU discover that your partner has different television-viewing patterns than you. He/she clings to the magic remote control like a vine and claims this object as his/her personal property, clicking away so quickly that you aren't sure what is on the television. When you finally get into a program, the channel is switched again. You feel the marriage is out of sync already. You:

A. Ask about this "clicker mania" phenomenon.

B. Suggest taking turns with the remote control.

C. Hide the remote control or take out the battery.

D. _____

11. YOU'VE SUFFERED THROUGH MORE THAN ONE of your partner's high school reunions. Your partner asks that you go to yet another one. You:

A. Plan to go and include a fun activity you would like to do during the weekend.

B. Act in a passive-aggressive manner and begrudgingly accompany your partner.

C. State that while you indeed love your partner, you don't love the reunions and would prefer not to go. (In the past, he/she ignored you at the reunions anyway.)

D. _____

12. YOU ANNOUNCE TO YOUR PARTNER THAT YOU have decided to make a lifetime dream come true and go to *Madame Butterfly*. He/she looks like a deer frozen in the car headlights and says he/she can't stand the thought of listening to opera for an entire evening. You:

A. Say that you were hoping to share this special event, but respect his/her decision not to go. You go alone or find someone else who loves the opera to join you.

B. Get into an argument about his/her decision and accuse him/her of never being supportive of your dreams.

C. Cop a resentment and refuse to go to an event that he/she expects to share with you.

D. _____

13. YOU AND YOUR PARTNER ARE HAVING A WON-derful time at a friend's wedding. The music begins, and you begin to hyperventilate. Dancing is your least favorite activity in the world. Your partner starts to move to the music, looks at you, and expects you to dance. You:

A. Excuse yourself, go straight to the bar to order a double, and hope that the alcohol helps loosen you up.

B. Ignore your partner and start a conversation with anyone standing nearby.

C. Say you would rather not dance and suggest he/she dance with someone else.

D. _____

14. YOU AND YOUR PARTNER ARE AT A WEDDING. The music begins. You can hardly wait to get out there and shake your booty. You:

A. Wait for your partner to ask, which never happens, and resent the fact that you didn't dance at all.

B. Share how important dancing is to you.

C. Ask your partner to dance and, if he/she refuses, look for opportunities to dance with others.

D. _____

15. THE WINTER WAS LONG. SPRING WAS DAMP AND cold. Finally, a free Saturday with a sunny forecast arrives! There is no doubt in your mind that the beach, sun, sand, and water are a winning combination. You discover that your partner's winning combination for the day is a couch, television, and baseball game. This difference of opinion poses a problem. You:

A. Give in, play the martyr, and sit by his/her side for sixteen innings of what you had planned on being only nine innings of punishment.

B. Suggest that your partner bring his/her cell phone with Internet capabilities to follow the game at the beach.

C. Support your partner's love of the game and tell him/her you are going to go to the beach.

D. _____

16. YOU AND YOUR PARTNER HAD WORKED HARD AT planning the wedding, and you are both excited about the honeymoon in Cancun. You look forward to a romantic, relaxing time. Your partner, on the other hand, has scheduled something to do each waking moment. You:

A. Share your goals and expectations and ask to work together on a schedule that satisfies both of your needs.

B. Say nothing and be a doormat.

C. Pout and stay in a resentful and bitter mood throughout the honeymoon.

D. _____

17. IT IS A BEAUTIFUL WEEKEND DAY, AND YOU suggest that you both head out for a hike. The trip to the mountain takes two hours, and in the past you have both really enjoyed the hiking experience. Your partner says he/she would rather not go. You:

A. Accuse him/her of being inconsiderate of your needs and of not loving you anymore.

B. Ask that your suggestion be reconsidered.

C. Accept his/her decision and then go hiking alone or with a friend.

D. _____

18. YOU AND YOUR PARTNER DECIDE TO GO SHOPPING on a rainy afternoon. Your partner does his/her shopping quickly and is ready to go home. You are now ready to shop. After a few minutes, he/she asks when you'll be finished. You are disappointed that your partner is totally bored by shopping, an activity you happen to love. You:

A. Are reminded that your partner has never enjoyed shopping, is not enjoying shopping, and presumably never will.

B. Go in and out of stores for hours.

C. Cut the trip short and plan on going alone or with a friend who likes to shop.

D. _____

19. YOU AND YOUR PARTNER ARE AT A PARTY AND are invited to join in a game of volleyball. Most people are there to have fun, but your partner seems to imagine that this is the gold medal match at the Olympics. You:

A. Are embarrassed by his/her aggressive, ego-driven behavior, but say nothing.

B. Make sarcastic comments to friends about your partner's competitive side and his/her inability to just relax and have fun.

C. Admit that you are a bit jealous of his/her athletic ability and try to accept his/her style of playing to win, but remind him/her of the unfriendliness of overcompetitive behavior.

D. _____

20. YOU ARE ON YOUR HONEYMOON, VISITING THE Louvre. You are anxious to get to the Impressionist section, which you have wanted to see since childhood. Your partner says he/she is ready to go. You say you want to see more. You:

A. Obediently leave with your partner.

B. Explain to your partner that you'd like to spend the remainder of the day at the museum since you've paid for admission and are interested in seeing the exhibits.

C. Assume that he/she doesn't have much appreciation for art and culture and is superficial.

D. _____

21. WHILE ON VACATION, YOUR PARTNER SUGGESTS going to a nearby lacrosse championship to see his/her alma mater play. You have never seen a game, don't know the rules, and are not a sports enthusiast. You:

A. Choose to go to be a good sport and make the most of it.

B. Opt out of going and hold a resentment about his/her decision to go to the game.

C. Question why some alumni can't let go of their school days.

D. _____

22. You decide to get involved with a local theater group, which will take up some free time. You:

A. Discuss your decision with your partner since it will affect the time that the two of you usually spend together.

B. Join the group and then let your partner know that you will not be home during rehearsal times.

C. Invite your partner to also join the group.

D. _____

23. You are excited about an upcoming holiday party. You:

A. Choose to attend whether or not your partner decides to go.

B. Expect your partner to go and be enthusiastic.

C. Decide not to go because your partner doesn't like social events.

D. _____

24. You come home from work and your partner is quiet. You sense something is wrong and ask if there is a problem. He/she states that he/she is very hurt and disappointed that you have forgotten that today is your wedding anniversary. You:

A. Lie, say that you did not forget, and say that you planned a surprise romantic dinner and evening out on the town.

B. Say "happy anniversary" and note that the date slipped your mind and continue with your own plans for the evening.

C. Admit that you forgot the special date, immediately write it on the calendar and in your daily planner, and suggest going out to celebrate your marriage.

D. _____

25. YOU BELIEVE IN THE PHILOSOPHY THAT AN
ounce of prevention is worth a pound of cure. One thing that bothers you is that you partner doesn't take good care of his/her car. You notice that the tires are bald before you get in the car to go on a planned trip. You are concerned about your safety and his/hers. You:

A. Submit your partner to a parental-like lecture on car care.

B. Raise the issue of safety and refuse to ride in the car until he/she gets new tires.

C. Say nothing, act like a victim, and put your safety at risk.

D. _____

26. YOU ARE GETTING READY TO GO WRAP SOME
gifts for a special occasion. You reach for the scissors, and they are not on the desk. Your partner isn't home, so you look around and find the scissors in the middle of his/her workshop projects. You:

A. Remind your partner that you would appreciate that he/she ask to borrow your belongings and then return them when finished.

B. Do the how-many-times-have-I-told-you-so speech.

C. Buy another pair of scissors especially for your partner.

D. _____

27. YOU AND YOUR PARTNER ARE BOTH INTERESTED
in world events, and reading the newspaper in the morning is a routine habit for both of you. You soon discover that your partner seems to claim ownership of the paper and then leaves sections of it throughout the house. You:

A. State your needs and suggest that you share the paper.

B. Order your own paper.

C. Say nothing and harbor frustration.

D. _____

28. YOUR PARTNER HAS ALWAYS SPENT A LOT of time with his/her best friend from childhood. Unfortunately, this friend is frequently included at family meals and social events. This friendship seems to be diverting your partner away from you and your marriage. You:

A. State your concern and ask your partner if he/she can try to see your perspective on the issue.

B. Say nothing and try to accept the choices your partner makes.

C. State that you think your partner spends way too much time with his/her friend and request that your partner decrease dinner invitations.

D. _____

29. YOU ARE IN THE MIDDLE OF AN ACTIVITY THAT requires focus and time spent alone. Your partner comes into the room to get something and begins to chat. In the past, you have clearly communicated that you need private time. You:

A. Explain that the closed door is an indication that you need quiet time and space.

B. Give a look that could kill, make a snide comment, and act in a passive-aggressive manner the rest of the evening.

C. Put a "Do Not Disturb" sign on the door.

D. _____

30. YOUR PARTNER HAS SURGERY. YOU:

A. Take the day off from work to spend time with him/her.

B. Call the hospital from work to see how things went.

C. Send flowers to your partner's hospital room and visit after work.

D. _____

31. YOUR PARTNER COMES HOME LATE ON FRIDAY night without calling and misses a special evening meal you had prepared. When you ask about the situation, he/she says he/she has a right to go out with the gang after work. You:

A. Say you understand wanting to go out, but would appreciate being informed of plans that may affect your evening.

B. Yell, scream, and blame him/her for ruining your evening.

C. Say that he/she missed curfew and is grounded.

D. _____

32. THERE IS A PILE OF MAIL ON THE TABLE AND one of your personal letters has been opened. You:

A. Calmly ask your partner if there is some explanation as to why your private mail was opened.

B. Confront your partner with the issue and state that you would appreciate that this not happen in the future.

C. Overreact and lecture your partner without hearing his/her explanation.

D. _____

33. YOU ARE ON THE PHONE WITH A FRIEND, AND you hear a click and realize your partner is listening in. You:

A. Ask your partner why this occurred during your phone conversation.

B. Rant, rave, and lecture about the evils of eavesdropping.

C. State your concern after the telephone call about lack of trust.

D. _____

34. WHILE CHECKING YOUR NEW E-MAILS YOU CAN see that they have already been read by someone else. You:

A. Assume that your partner read the e-mails since he/she is the only other person who knows your password. You then ask your partner if he/she has, in fact, read your e-mails.

B. Say nothing and change your password.

C. Hack into his/her e-mail account whenever you feel like it.

D. _____

35. THE ALLOTTED NUMBER OF MINUTES ON THE cell phone account has been exceeded on your partner's phone, and you wonder who he/she has been talking with. You:

A. Show your partner the bill and ask why the number of minutes have increased.

B. Go online to check the account and secretly check his/her phone for incoming and outgoing numbers.

C. Leave the bill on the kitchen table with a note that you expect him/her to pay the extra amount.

D. _____

36. YOUR PARTNER HAS A JOURNAL AND YOU ARE curious about what he/she has written in it. You:

A. Use positive affirmations, like "My partner is entitled to his/her privacy and I would be wrong to invade his/her privacy," to resist the temptation of peeking.

B. Ask your partner what he/she writes about.

C. Regularly read the journal.

D. _____

37. IT'S YOUR BIRTHDAY, AND YOU ARE LOOKING

forward to a celebration. You wait for a "happy birthday" greeting from your partner, but you receive none . . . all day. You are sad and angry at the same time. You:

A. Give a stern lecture on the importance of remembering birthdays and special occasions in the marriage relationship.

B. Share your feelings honestly, tell him/her that celebrating birthdays is important to you, and request that he/she write the date on his/her calendar and acknowledge the special day.

C. Say nothing, and ignore his/her next birthday.

D. _____

CHAPTER FIVE

FAMILY AND FRIENDS

"A good marriage is one which allows for change and growth in the individuals and in the way they express their love."

—PEARL S. BUCK

We share precious life events with our partner, family, and friends. Each partner brings to a marriage various memories, traditions, and learned behaviors, and conflicts may occur due to differences in preferences in social activities and family gatherings. Remember that no two people think the exact same thoughts or have the same behaviors. Differences are normal. To walk through married life and balance time with both families with love and respect requires clear communication, patience, and willingness to occasionally compromise. The following examples present some typical social situations concerning family and friends:

I. YOU RUN INTO A FRIEND YOU HAVEN'T SEEN IN a while who fills you in on the great party held on the previous Saturday night. She asks why you never returned an RSVP. You realize your partner never gave you the message, and you missed a good time with friends. You:

A. Tell your partner that you would appreciate being given your phone messages in the future.

B. Put pens and pads of paper next to each phone and suggest he/she write down messages.

C. Don't say a word and conveniently "forget" to give him/her phone messages.

D. _____

2. THE HOLIDAYS ARE DRAWING NEAR. FOR YEARS
you have shouldered the responsibility for taking the time and energy to buy the gifts you both give. Your time is more limited now, and you have begun to dread the onset of the holiday season. You:

A. Make a unilateral decision to give only gift certificates.

B. Ask your partner that he/she help with the gift lists and shopping.

C. Feel guilty and go back into overdrive.

D. _____

3. YOUR PARTNER INFORMS YOU THAT YOU BOTH
have been invited to a work-related party, but you are given no details. Weeks later, you are informed that the party is the next day, a day that you had made plans to do something special on your own. You:

A. Go ahead with your own plans since your partner did not give you specific information about the party ahead of time.

B. Ask your partner to get more information about the party's time and the place in hopes you could attend both events.

C. Cancel your plans, go to the event, and tell everyone that your partner never gets anything right and spoiled your plans for the day.

D. _____

4. YOU HAVE BEEN INVITED TO PLAY DOUBLES WITH
new neighbors. Your tennis skills are average, and your partner's are above average. You like to have fun when you play. Your partner likes to win. You both plan game strategy ahead of time. The match begins, your

"teammate" poaches throughout, diving in front of you for everything that goes over the net. You:

A. Ask how and why the strategy decided upon had been changed.

B. Let him/her know that you would rather not play doubles because you are in it for fun, not just to win.

C. Say nothing, smile, and never play tennis with him/her again.

D. _____

5. IT IS THE HOLIDAY SEASON ONCE AGAIN AND anxiety has set in. You and your partner are headed to visit your in-laws for a long weekend. From the time of your arrival to the time of your departure, everyone is in the hugging mode. As much as you have tried to adapt to this demonstrative form of affection, you are used to family gatherings where hugging is kept to a minimum. You:

A. Tell your partner that all of the "closeness" makes you uncomfortable because your family almost never shows affection.

B. Stay in a state of anxiety all weekend long, get passive-aggressive, and put a damper on the holiday for yourself and your partner.

C. Go to a counselor or talk to friend and ask for advice.

D. _____

6. YOU'VE BEEN WAITING FOR A SPECIAL SOCIAL event. Your partner starts to act sick and says he/she is not up to going out. You:

A. Go anyway, despite the fact that you are disappointed that your partner won't attend.

B. React with anger to this recurring "ailment," which you suspect is a convenient excuse to avoid being social.

C. Cut your partner some slack and respect his/her decision.

D. _____

7. SOMEONE YOU CARE ABOUT DIES, AND YOU ASK your partner to go to the wake and funeral. He/she looks at you with a puzzled expression and says "no" because he/she didn't even know the person. You:

A. Say nothing, go to the wake and funeral alone, and feel sad and resentful that your partner is not there to support you when you need him/her the most.

B. State that you need and want support during this time of loss.

C. Call a friend or relative and ask them to go with you.

D. _____

8. THERE WAS NO MENTION IN THE MARRIAGE VOWS about your partner's Saturday golf game. Before marriage and soon after the honeymoon, golf was not a priority. Saturdays were spent together, doing fun activities or house-related chores. After the vows, the weekend golf pattern slowly evolved. You:

A. Nag, whine, and complain each week, trying to make your partner feel guilty.

B. Say you understand his/her intense love of the sport, but that you'd like to spend some Saturdays doing an activity together.

C. Find something you like to do on your own or with friends on Saturdays.

D. _____

9. ON YOUR HONEYMOON, YOU AND YOUR PARTNER talk about how grateful you are for all of the wedding gifts you received. You mention the issue of thank-you notes and ask how this task will be accomplished. Your partner states that this is not his/her department and expects you to write all of the notes. You:

A. Kindly explain that thanking guests for "our" wedding gifts is "our" responsibility.

B. Agree that writing thank-you notes is a pain in the neck and bag the idea.

C. Suggest making a plan to work together to make the task a bit more pleasant.

D. _____

10. YOU'VE MOVED INTO AN APARTMENT/HOUSE and are anxious to create a comfortable, stylish home. You begin the task of decorating, and your partner gets upset that you did not even discuss the issue with him/her. You:

A. Recognize that you have not acted in a cooperative manner and state that you are open to the process of planning the decorating project together.

B. State that you have better taste in color and design and continue to control the situation.

C. Distance yourself from any decorating because your plan was interrupted.

D. _____

11. YOUR PARTNER WANTS A DOG. YOU WOULD PRE-fer a cat. Then, one day your partner surprises you with a puppy. You:

A. Melt and welcome the puppy without thinking of what the consequences and responsibilities will be.

B. React in a fit of rage because such a major decision was done unilaterally.

C. State you are not ready for a pet until all of the details of responsibility, such as feeding, cleaning, walking, vet visits, and vet bills, have been worked out.

D. _____

12. YOU HAVE SPENT PREVIOUS THANKSGIVINGS

with your own family. While at dinner, your mother-in-law says she is looking forward to spending the upcoming holiday with you. You quickly realize that your partner made plans without you, and was insensitive to the fact that you were planning on spending the holiday with your own family. You are livid about your partner's decision. You:

A. Let your partner know that you feel upset, angry, and hurt that he/she did not talk this over before making plans.

B. Go to his/her family's home and resent each moment.

C. Discuss the situation and plan a strategy, such as alternating the holiday visits between families.

D. _____

13. YOU HAVE A CHANCE TO GET TOGETHER WITH

old friends about once a month. You mention an upcoming get-together, and your partner accuses you of "always" going out with friends. You:

A. Feel guilty and choose not to see your friends anymore.

B. Overreact, say things you later regret, slam the door, and walk out.

C. Explain that this get-together is an important social activity for you and state where you're going and when you'll return.

D. _____

14. TOO MANY SATURDAY NIGHTS HAVE BEEN SPENT

at home, and it seems like you and your partner don't have much of a social life. You:

A. Do and say nothing because you just don't have the energy to get people together.

B. Blame your partner for the boring social situation.

C. Work with your partner to make a plan to get out more regularly.

D. _____

15. YOUR PARENTS ARE COMING TO VISIT, AND
you're looking forward to their stay. Your partner seems edgy about their
arrival and says that a week is a long time for company to visit. You:

A. Commit to keeping them busy with activities.

B. Take his/her response personally.

C. Assure your partner that it is not unusual to be apprehensive
when in-laws visit,

D. _____

16. YOU HAVE A FIGHT WITH YOUR PARTNER AND
immediately call one of your parents. Your spouse hears the conversation
and is upset at you for discussing personal issues. You:

A. Tell him/her it is your right to say what you want to anyone.

B. Say that you needed an objective, caring ear to listen to you.

C. Say that you did not know that you might have done something
inconsiderate that may have broken his/her trust.

D. _____

17. YOU MET YOUR PARTNER AT YOUR FATHER'S
business, where he/she had been recently hired. During the planning of
the wedding and since, your partner keeps telling stories of how your
father is overworking him/her. You:

A. Feel torn between your father and partner yet don't say anything
about the situation.

B. Suggest that your partner schedule a meeting to voice concerns about
the workload.

C. Point out that if the problem continues, it may be best for everyone
if your partner gets a job elsewhere to avoid family conflicts.

D. _____

18. THE PHONE RINGS OFTEN AND AT ALL HOURS OF the day and night. Your partner is very social, and the constant phone calls are becoming a nuisance. You:

A. Say nothing.

B. Request that no calls be accepted after 11 p.m. because you need your sleep.

C. Say something sarcastic when the phone rings.

D. _____

19. IT'S SATURDAY. YOU HAVE HAD A ROUGH WEEK, and just want to rest. Suddenly, two of your partner's friends/relatives arrives at the door unannounced. You:

A. Refuse to answer the door.

B. Invite them in and let them know that you are taking a day of rest and relaxation.

C. Suggest to your partner that he/she entertain the unexpected guests.

D. _____

20. YOUR PARTNER SPENDS MOST EVENINGS OUT with his/her friends doing sporting and political activities. You:

A. Blame your partner for making you feel left out.

B. Suggest that you set at least one evening aside for a "date" with one another.

C. Choose to spend the time doing something you would enjoy with people you would like to be with.

D. _____

21. You invite your family over to your house
to celebrate your parent's anniversary. Unbeknownst to you, your sister has already made plans for the event and you are upset. You:

A. Vent about the issue and thank your partner for listening.

B. Ask your partner for advice about what to do about the situation.

C. Take out your anger on him/her.

D. _____

22. There's a "Jack and Jill" shower for one
of your cousins, and your partner refuses to go. You:

A. Ask your partner to reconsider because family gatherings are important to you.

B. Accept your partner's decision, no questions asked.

C. Lecture your partner on the responsibilities of married life.

D. _____

23. Family connections are important to you,
and you cannot understand why your partner doesn't call or visit his/her family as often as you visit yours. You:

A. Don't say anything, but obsess about it.

B. Ask your partner why there doesn't seem to be much communication or many visits with his/her family.

C. Suggest that your partner take steps to get closer to his/her family.

D. _____

CHAPTER SIX:

BALANCING SEX, INTIMACY, AND PERSONAL BOUNDARIES

"Let there be spaces in your togetherness."

—KHALIL GIBRAN

Sharing time, living space, personal belongings, and physical self with your marriage partner are major adjustments that take time, patience, and unconditional love. The most important element and common thread in trying to balance sex, intimacy, and personal boundaries is respect. There needs to be consideration of the other person's feelings, belongings, and physical being.

The challenge is to work things out by clearly stating your wants and needs while respecting the wants and needs of your partner by creating guidelines and boundaries within the marriage that ensure personal privacy. Crossing personal boundaries can cause hurt and resentment. A few simple guidelines to keep in mind are: Respect the other person's desires and fears related to sex; treat the other person the way you would like to be treated; and request permission to use any of their personal belongings. The following examples take into account some situations that relate to intimacy and trust:

1. A sign that the honeymoon may well be over: You come to bed dressed in fleece warm-ups and socks because you are cold. Your partner asks about this new attire and accuses you of looking like an old-timer. You:

A. Tell him/her that you feel frozen and are dressed for warmth.

B. Suggest buying an extra comforter or a dual-controlled electric blanket.

C. Don't say a word and turn away.

D. _____

2. You have been back a few weeks from the honeymoon and are getting into the groove of married life. You have enjoyed the intimacy that wedded life has brought, but your partner seems to want to be intimate morning, noon, and night. You have responsibilities to take care of, and sometimes you just need a good night's sleep. You:

A. Use the old "I've got a headache" line.

B. Ask to talk about the issue.

C. Obediently comply with his/her wishes.

D. _____

3. Your partner awaits you in a warm, relaxing bathtub. The business phone rings. You:

A. Answer the phone and discuss business, therefore missing the intimate experience.

B. Choose not to answer the phone yet obsess about the missed phone call nonetheless.

C. Choose not to answer the phone, knowing that whoever called can leave a message.

D. _____

4. YOU ACCIDENTALLY DISCOVER THAT YOUR PARTNER has been spending time watching pornography on the Internet. At the same time, he/she hasn't shown much interest in having sex with you. You:

A. Say nothing, yet feel rejected.

B. Calmly let your partner know what you discovered and ask for an explanation.

C. Constantly check up on your partner when he/she is on the computer and after he/she logs off.

D. _____   _____

5. YOUR PARTNER HAS BEEN SPENDING SEVERAL hours on the computer each evening and on weekends, and you discover that he/she spends time in chat rooms and e-mailing people he/she met online. You:

A. Tell yourself that this is normal and that you shouldn't be upset, though you are.

B. Open your partner's e-mails to make sure there is nothing suspicious going on.

C. Reveal your discovery to your partner and share the fear that this behavior may be inappropriate in a marriage.

D. _____

6. YOU ARE AT A PARTY WITH OLD FRIENDS AND YOUR ex is there. You spend a while talking about the "good old times" and your spouse is sent into a jealous rage on the way home in the car. You:

A. Explain that this person means nothing to you now and indicate that you'll be more sensitive in the future.

B. Describe your partner's response as immature and ridiculous.

c. Let your partner know that you did not realize that this behavior was so hurtful, and promise to avoid spending any length of time in the future with your ex.

D. _____

7. You've had a horrendous day at work. It's your turn to cook dinner, and your partner glides through the door and begins to make sexual advances. You:

A. Drop everything and have sex out of some kind of duty, which is not enjoyable.

B. Chastise your partner for being in a good mood and for not knowing that you are totally stressed-out.

c. Put down the dishes, choose to spend intimate time together, and then ask for some help to prepare dinner.

D. _____

8. You have a monstrous headache, and your partner suggests having sex. You:

A. Calmly announce that you have a terrible headache and need to be left alone.

B. Ask that instead of sex, your partner massage your temples and hold you near.

c. Accuse your partner of being insensitive for not reading your mind and recognizing that you are in pain.

D. _____

9. You are on a weekend getaway and spending the night in a hotel. Your partner can't wait to have sex. You were given an adjoining room at the hotel, and you feel uptight about the extra door. You:

A. State your concern and refuse to have sex.

B. Make sure that the door is securely locked.

C. Enjoy the mini-vacation. Leave your troubles behind, get back in touch with your partner, and next time request a room that is not adjoining.

D. _____

10. **YOUR IN-LAWS ARE VISITING, AND AS YOU CLIMB** into bed, you let your partner know that you are in the mood for love. Your partner refuses your advances because there are other people in the house. You:

A. Kindly inform your partner that his/her parents actually had sex and he/she is proof of that.

B. Say you understand, but wonder how you will last without sex for the weeklong duration of their visit.

C. Suggest closing the door tightly and turning up the radio or television to muffle any sounds of passion.

D. _____

11. **YOU AND YOUR PARTNER WOULD LIKE TO START** a family in a year or two. Thus far in your relationship, there is no definite birth control plan in place. You:

A. Take care of this responsibility on your own.

B. Put off bringing up the subject because there have been arguments about it in the past.

C. Tell your partner that this issue needs to be addressed immediately because you need to know where he/she stands on the issue before getting married.

D. _____

12. IN THE MIDDLE OF THE NIGHT, YOUR PARTNER wakes you up with a romantic serenade. You:

A. Roll over and pretend that you missed what happened.

B. Give a lecture on the importance of getting a good night's sleep.

C. Feel the attraction and share a wonderful middle-of-the-night romp.

D. _____

13. YOU WOKE UP, LOOKED AT YOUR PARTNER, and wanted to make love. Though it is a workday, there is time for a quickie. You:

A. Tell your partner how attractive he/she is and say that you want to show your love.

B. Say nothing because you are afraid of being rejected.

C. Expect that your partner will feel the same way and do what you demand.

D. _____

14. YOU AND YOUR PARTNER CAME FROM VERY different backgrounds. Sex was discussed in your partner's family. The word was not spoken in your family. Now that you are married (or planning on having sex before marriage), you are not sure how to proceed. You:

A. Talk about your insecurity with your partner and ask that the two of you discuss the issues surrounding intimacy.

B. Look for books and ask friends questions about what a healthy sex life is like.

C. Continue to play the "naive" role; maybe that is what your partner wants.

D. _____

15. YOU WONDER HOW YOU AND YOUR PARTNER

will keep the love light of passion burning over the years. You:

A. Do some reading and research.

B. Tell your partner what you would like your romantic, intimate life to be like, and ask your partner to verbalize his/her vision of intimacy.

C. Say and do nothing, preferring to just wait and see what happens.

D. _____

16. YOU LOVE DANCING AND CANDLELIGHT. IN YOUR

mind, romance is the link to intimacy. You thought your partner felt the same way, but there is something missing. You:

A. Sarcastically hint that he/she is missing the boat.

B. Create a romantic mood with dinner, candlelight, and music, and see how your partner responds.

C. Honestly explain to your partner that you require a little bit of romance to get you into an intimate mood.

D. _____

17. YOU ARE NOT SURE WHAT YOUR PARTNER WANTS

in bed. You:

A. Ask what he/she would prefer.

B. Try what you think would work.

C. Wait for your partner to tell you what he/she wants.

D. _____

18. YOU ARE NOT SURE WHAT TO SAY DURING SEX,

and your partner is saying things you don't like hearing. You:

A. Ask for a discussion about how to better relate verbally in intimate situations.

B. Get angry at the way you were spoken to and take it out on your partner.

C. Ask your partner what he/she would like to hear and ask your partner to speak to you in a way that is comfortable to you.

D. _____

19. Your partner likes the lights on. You like the lights off. You:

A. Suggest a compromise, like candlelight.

B. Let your partner know why you prefer darkness.

C. Refuse to have sex with the lights on.

D. _____

20. You don't need music or dancing; you just need sex often. You wonder why your partner is not in the same mode. You:

A. Explain that you have a strong sexual desire that occurs often and you would like to share that beautiful intimacy.

B. Expect that your partner do as told whenever you desire sex.

C. Wait for an advance from your partner.

D. _____

21. Your partner has stated some sexual preferences that you are not comfortable with. You:

A. Say that you are normally uncomfortable trying something new, but are willing to be open to his/her needs.

B. Ask more specific questions.

C. Say absolutely no, never.

D. _____

22. YOU AND YOUR PARTNER ARE TAKING A STROLL.
It is dusk and downright romantic. You reach out to hold his/her hand.
His/her response is discomfort and tightened muscles. A moment later he/
she lets go of your hand, changes the subject, and points at something
to divert your attention. You feel disappointed because you really enjoy
holding hands. It is a normal activity in a healthy relationship. You:

A. Wonder if he/she loves you anymore.

B. Criticize his/her response, which killed the mood.

C. Wait for an opportune time to bring up the subject, and ask why holding hands in public feels uncomfortable to him/her.

D. _____

23. DURING COURTING DAYS, YOUR PARTNER OFTEN
kissed you in public. Once you got married, the novelty wore off, and he/
she rarely kisses you in public. You:

A. Ask why kissing has waned, and wonder if there is someone else in
your partner's life.

B. Take the initiative: When the spirit moves you, give your partner a
kiss in public.

C. State that you have a need to feel free to show affection in and out
of the home.

D. _____

24. YOU ARE IN THE BATHTUB. THE DOOR OPENS,
and you feel your privacy has been invaded. You:

A. Lash out and give a lecture about knocking first.

B. Let your partner know that you would appreciate privacy.

C. Lock the door when in the bath to avoid having your privacy invaded.

D. _____

25. YOU SEE A ROMANTIC THRILLER ABOUT AN
affair, which leaves you feeling upset and a bit paranoid. You:

A. Check your partner's computer files, phone records, credit card statements, and mileage on his/her car.

B. Let your partner know that the film upset you and has caused a fear of marriage problems. Then ask your partner to let you know that he/she is faithful and can be trusted.

C. Say nothing and live in fear and anxiety.

D. _____

26. YOU LIKE SLEEPING NAKED AND WISH YOUR
partner would do the same because there is nothing like the feeling of skin to skin. You:

A. Don't say anything, assuming that this might be too much to ask.

B. Let your partner know your desire.

C. Label your partner "frigid" if he/she will not go along with your idea.

D. _____

CHAPTER SEVEN

MONEY, MONEY, MONEY

"A good marriage is a contest of generosity."

—DIANE SAWYER

Financial problems can be a leading cause of conflict in a marriage, and may even cause divorce. For example, the ease of using credit cards has the potential of creating sizable debts, which can cause major credit problems and put stress on the marriage relationship. Clear, honest communication is an important part of working together to deal with the financial issues in a marriage.

Since money plays such a major role in everyday life, it makes sense that partners look at all details related to money, share their goals and expectations, and work together to create a successful financial plan.

Taking the time to work out money issues assures that both partners are on the same page from the beginning. If finances are not discussed beforehand, they will eventually move to the forefront. Working out budget and financial issues are just a part of everyday life, month after month, year after year—barring those individuals who are fortunate enough to have enough money not to ever have to worry.

Even when couples go over every financial detail, there will always be unexpected expenses or unexpected situations, such as: higher rent, car problems, or the loss of a job. When these unexpected money crises occur, couples have the choice of getting upset and letting the situation get them off balance, or accepting that these situations occur, and remaining centered and dedicated to working together to solve the problem. Nonetheless, a few of the basic situations that every couple should be prepared for are:

- Who is responsible for writing out checks?
- Will there be a joint account and/or separate accounts?
- What percentage of income will go toward household bills and savings?
- Will the tax refund be saved or spent?

Here are some typical situations and options to serve as reminders that after the honeymoon is over, bills are a reality that need to be dealt with:

1. YOUR SPOUSE DECIDES TO JOIN A FITNESS CLUB. The club's cost is very high, and you immediately worry that its fee may break the budget. You:

A. Say nothing and continue to worry, which gets in the way of the relationship.

B. Suggest having a meeting to discuss how to manage this new monthly payment.

C. Give a parental lecture on how selfish it is to spend money on oneself when the budget is tight.

D. _____

2. MEDICAL INSURANCE IS NOT INCLUDED IN EITHER of your or your partner's job benefits. This is a major concern to you, yet your partner doesn't see this as being a priority. You:

A. Suggest that one or both of you begin looking for a job with health benefits.

B. Suggest that you both try to find affordable health insurance.

c. Verbally attack your partner and blame him/her for not taking care of this important issue.

D. _____

3. THE CREDIT CARD BILL ARRIVES, AND YOU CAN
plainly see that your partner has been spending so much money that that card's limit has almost been reached. You:

A. Show your anger by yelling.

B. Take time to mellow out a bit, and then ask to set some time aside to talk about the finances.

c. Tell your partner that he/she is responsible for any debts incurred.

D. _____

4. YOUR SPOUSE HAS BEEN CORRALLED BY A
suave insurance agent who has tried to sell a large insurance policy on you. You:

A. Honestly let your partner know that you feel creeped out by the agent's tactics.

B. Ask to learn more about insurance investments before you sign anything.

c. Go on and on about how insurance is all just a waste of money.

D. _____

5. YOU CAN GET TWO TICKETS TO THE WORLD
Series for $500. This is a once-in-a-lifetime opportunity. You:

A. Buy the tickets without discussing the issue; after all, this is a once-in-a-lifetime opportunity.

B. Invite your partner to join you. If he/she declines, invite a close friend instead.

c. Pass up the opportunity because you feel guilty spending that much money on a game.

D. _____

6. You love movies and decide to upgrade the
cable/satellite package without consulting your partner. Your partner overreacts. You:

A. Let it be known that you are the head of the house and can order what you want.

B. Apologize for not discussing the issue, and ask that it be considered by both of you.

C. Do not allow your partner to watch any of the movies offered by the new package.

D. _____

7. You love your MP3 player and listen to
music a lot. This is your hobby and you collect all kinds of music. Your partner is upset at the amount of money being spent on your hobby. You:

A. Tell your partner it is not his/her business and to stop bugging you.

B. Look at the amount of money spent to determine if the amount is reasonable or not.

C. Offer to share some of the music, especially the kind that your partner prefers.

D. _____

8. You just can't resist watching and ordering
from a home shopping network. You notice that you are on a first-name basis with the UPS carrier and recognize that you may have become a shopaholic. You:

A. Tell your partner that you have spent too much money shopping and ask for help.

B. Let your partner know that you have a problem, will take care of current charges, and will try to resist the temptation to buy additional products.

C. Keep shopping because it makes you feel good.

D. _____

9. DUE TO BUSY SCHEDULES AND LACK OF FREE time, you and your partner choose to dine out frequently. Neither of you likes to cook, and neither takes on the responsibility, yet the credit card balances continue to grow. You:

A. Do nothing about the problem because you are too tired to deal with it.

B. Take to worrying and obsessing about the problem and try to find a solution on your own.

C. State that there is a financial problem related to eating out so often and suggest having a meeting to brainstorm about how to change this pattern.

D. _____

10. YOUR PARTNER ANNOUNCES THE DECISION TO buy a new SUV. The cost seems high, and you have no idea how you both will pay for it. You:

A. Point your finger at your partner and grill him/her on what you consider inconsiderate and irresponsible marital behavior.

B. Overreact in a hurtful way to punish your partner's thoughtlessness.

C. Cool off and calmly explain that you both agreed to discuss any large financial decisions.

D. _____

11. YOUR PARTNER SUGGESTS GETTING ONE JOINT
bank account for both of you. You would rather keep one joint account for shared costs and a separate account for personal items. You:

A. Criticize your partner for trying to control all the money.

B. State that it is important for you to keep a separate account for your own well-being.

C. Do what your partner wants you to do.

D. _____

12. THE WEDDING AND HONEYMOON WERE FABULOUS,
and married life is wonderful. Weeks go by, bills come in, and since there was no discussion about who would pay for what when, the bills remain unpaid. All of a sudden, reality hits and you don't know what to do. You:

A. Call a meeting to discuss the finances and to create a plan that includes how the bills will be paid regularly.

B. Fall apart and blame your partner for his/her inaction.

C. Take immediate action and begin to pay the bills.

D. _____

13. IT'S TIME TO PAY THE BILLS, AND THE CHECKBOOK
and stamps are nowhere to be found. Worse, the bills, envelopes, and return labels are scattered in different places. This confusion causes anxiety and frustration. You:

A. Suggest establishing a location to keep everything related to finances in one place.

B. Complain, but do nothing to change the situation.

C. Ask your partner for help organizing paperwork and paying the bills.

D. _____

14. YOU WORK FULL TIME WHILE YOUR PARTNER

attends school full time and incurs debt. Though you agreed to financially support your partner, you feel "used" and unappreciated and are resentful that you are working to pay the bills. You:

A. Say nothing and seethe inside.

B. Speak to your partner from the heart and let him/her know how you feel. Discuss the plan and see if there are ways to adapt or change it so as to alleviate your financial burden.

C. Accept your feelings and remind yourself that school will last a finite time and there will be financial help from your partner coming in after graduation.

D. _____

15. A LARGE UNEXPECTED BILL COMES IN AND

there is little extra money to pay the total. You:

A. Volunteer to find a part-time job to pick up the slack for the short term.

B. Call a meeting and work together to figure out how to pay the bill.

C. Ignore it and assume that your partner will take care of it.

D. _____

16. YOU AND YOUR PARTNER HEAD OUT FOR A

beautiful day at the racetrack. He/she becomes obsessed with winning and believes there is a profit to be made by betting big. Race after race, there are no winnings, but there is a big dent on the credit card. You:

A. Clearly state that you are disappointed in both your partner's gambling and his/her loss of money.

B. Never again suggest a visit to the racetrack or the casino for a day of fun.

c. Hope that he/she never gets involved with the stock market or poker.

D. _____

17. YOUR PARTNER WORKS ON WALL STREET AND IS obsessed with playing the market. The problem is that there is rarely a profit, and there isn't enough money to pay bills for the month. You:

A. State that there is a problem with cash flow and ask to discuss the problem and come up with a strategy to pay this month's bills.

B. Lecture your partner on his/her irresponsible behavior.

c. Suggest that your partner look into getting some sound advice in safer investment opportunities.

D. _____

18. YOU WOULD LIKE TO GO ON AN ANNUAL VACATION, but are unsure of whether or not your partner has the same desire. You:

A. Openly and honestly let your partner know that you love taking vacations and would like to be able to take one every year.

B. Make vacation plans on a whim without consulting your partner.

c. Create a financial and time plan that would allow for an annual vacation and then present the idea to your partner for consideration.

D. _____

19. AFTER SEEING ADS ON TELEVISION FOR MORTGAGE rates, you have a desire to buy a home. You:

A. Tell your partner that you expect to buy a home as soon as possible and begin by saving every penny.

B. Ask your partner what he/she envisions for future living arrangements.

c. Call the realtor to start looking, even though there isn't enough money for a down payment and your partner isn't on board.

D. _____

20. Whenever you go out to dinner with friends, your partner picks up the tab. Though a nice gesture, this common occurrence is building up the credit card debt. You:

A. Tell your partner that this kind of behavior is unacceptable.

B. Clearly let your partner know that this may be kind, but explain that people generally pay for their share of meals.

C. The next time you go out to a restaurant, you request that your partner refrain from paying the full bill.

D. _____

21. It is springtime, the open road is calling, and all you want to do is buy a motorcycle and ride like the wind. You:

A. Go directly to the nearest dealership and buy one.

B. Request a meeting with your partner to discuss this possible purchase, with a financial plan in hand.

C. Take a bit of time to look at the pros and cons before making a purchase or bringing up the subject with your partner.

D. _____

22. There is a check missing in the joint account, with no amount listed. You:

A. Yell, scream, and give a lecture about financial management.

B. Take the checkbook away.

C. Discuss the issue at a convenient time in a calm manner.

D. _____

23. You forgot to enter a check amount in the ledger. Your partner asks if you wrote out a check and, if so, what the amount was. When you say that you forgot to enter the check, you are criticized for "never doing anything right." You:

A. React by feeling hurt and showing your anger at the accusation.

B. Admit that you make mistakes and request that you not be criticized.

C. Get carbon checks, which should solve the problem.

D. _____

24. AT THE END OF THE YEAR, YOU SUGGEST THAT you file the income tax return early. You start preparing documents and receipts and ask for your partner's financial information for the prior year. January comes and goes, as does February, March, and the beginning of April. You ask again and are told not to worry and that it is no big deal. On April 14, your partner is totally stressed-out, voices frustration at you, stays up all night calculating the taxes, and files for an extension. You:

A. Let your partner know that verbal abuse will not be tolerated and request that you be treated with respect.

B. File separately the next year. Even if the cost is higher, it's worth the peace of mind.

C. Ask that the issue be discussed earlier next year in the hopes of making the process go smoother the next time around.

D. _____

CHAPTER EIGHT

HELPFUL HINTS OR ATTACKS?

"Marriage is an adventure, like going to war."

—GILBERT K. CHESTERTON

In a marriage, couples discuss just about everything under the sun. Opinions are traded on issues ranging from what color to paint the kitchen to a new location for a job. Statements of disagreement or opposite opinions may come across as hurtful and manipulative. Hearing negative comments may be difficult and cause negative responses. Being prepared for and accepting these kind of normal personal differences and the existence of occasional conflict in a marriage helps each partner choose a positive rather than a negative response.

One common communication misunderstanding is when a partner listens to a problem the other is dealing with and immediately gives advice about how to solve the problem. This unsolicited advice may be interpreted as patronizing or insulting.

Another pitfall is when one partner notices something about the other person that he/she thinks should be changed. The subject could range from style of clothes to road rage. In the process of trying to be helpful, the comment may instead be hurtful.

In each case, the message was meant to be positive, but somehow came across as negative. Being honest about hurt feelings and other negative emotions can improve the relationship and avoid negative situations.

The following examples are comprised of direct comments, some positive and some negative, from one partner to the other. A wide variety of responses is offered to cope with helpful hints as well as criticism:

1. "I AM SO UPSET. I DIDN'T SLEEP AT ALL LAST night. Your loud snoring kept me awake all night." Your response could be:

A. Next time wake me up and I'll turn on my side. That might stop the snoring.

B. You could have slept on the couch.

C. If this is such a problem, I'll do some research and try to get some help to stop snoring.

D. _____

2. "I AM TIRED OF YOU WORKING LATE. YOUR JOB seems to have taken priority over our marriage." Your response could be:

A. I didn't realize how many hours I have been working. I'll try to cut back.

B. I am on a deadline, and when the project is over, my schedule will be back to the normal hours.

C. Grow up. You can't have everything you want all the time.

D. _____

3. "THE HOUSE, CAR, AND ALL OF MY CLOTHES smell like a smokestack. You have to stop smoking." Your response could be:

A. I'll do as I please.

B. You have a point. It is not a healthy habit, and I'll try to stop.

C. I just can't seem to stop. But I will agree to smoke outside from now on.

D. _____

4. "WE ARE LATE AGAIN FOR THE MOVIES, AND IT IS all your fault. What is wrong with you that you cannot ever be on time?" Your response could be:

A. It's genetic. No one in my family is on time.

B. If you don't like it, then take your own car and get yourself there on time.

C. Can you help me try to break this longstanding habit?

D. _____   _____

5. "THERE'S NO FOOD IN THE REFRIGERATOR. What's for supper?" Your response could be:

A. How about you go grocery shopping for a change?

B. Let's go out for a quick meal and then go grocery shopping and stock up on some food.

C. We can always order pizza, again.

D. _____

6. "THE BANK CALLED, AND THE ACCOUNT IS WAY overdrawn. I am angry at you for being so careless with money." Your response could be:

A. This is the first time I have caused any overdrafts. I'll pay the fee.

B. It's no big deal.

C. You may be angry, but I would appreciate that you don't yell at me. I will take care of the problem tomorrow.

D. _____

7. "YOU PROMISED TO PAINT THE KITCHEN LAST year; I can't stand looking at these dingy walls any longer. When will you take care of this?" Your response could be:

A. I may have promised, but I have been busy. Maybe we could hire someone to paint or you could paint the kitchen yourself.

B. Get off my back. I'll do it when I am good and ready.

C. I decided I don't want to paint the kitchen after all.

D. _____

8. "IF YOU DON'T START EXERCISING, YOU'LL GET heart disease." Your response could be:

A. You aren't a fortune-teller. I may never get heart disease.

B. Good idea. How about taking a walk with me right now?

C. I do not appreciate your suggestions when they come across as being patronizing.

D. _____

9. "I HAVE BEGGED THAT WE GO ON A VACATION, and you keep putting it off. I really need a vacation and have scheduled one for the end of next month. You're invited to join me, but I am going even if you choose not to." Your response could be:

A. You have no right to go on your own, and I refuse to go.

B. Push has come to shove. I'll try to get the time off.

C. Funny you bring up vacation . . . I feel like I need one as soon as possible. Thank you. We will have such fun.

D. _____

10. "SINCE YOU CONTINUE TO WORK LATE INTO the evenings, I have signed up for some night classes." Your response could be:

A. Sorry about not getting home earlier, but there is too much to do at work. It's fine with me that you take the classes.

B. You should stay home at night where you belong.

C. It is a good idea to sign up for classes, but I wish we could have discussed the issue before you made these plans.

D. _____

11. "MY JOB HAS JUST BEEN TRANSFERRED ACROSS the country. We have to move there in three months." Your response could be:

A. It sounds like you have made a decision on your own about where our home will be. I suggest that we talk this through and come to a decision together.

B. You may be moving across the country and leaving family, friends, familiar places, and our home, but I am not going anywhere.

C. This is a shock. We'll have to work through this together and make plans to move.

D. _____

12. "YOU KEEP GAINING WEIGHT. DON'T YOU CARE about what you look like?" Your response could be:

A. I don't know how to lose this weight. Maybe we could make some changes in our diet and exercise.

B. Mind your own business.

C. Thanks for the wake-up call. Of course I am concerned. I guess I will need to do something about getting into shape, rather than just talking about it.

D. _____

13. "I CAN'T STAND IT ANYMORE, YOU TALK NONSTOP. I need to go into another room for some quiet." Your response could be:

A. You have really hurt my feelings. You could have been a bit kinder when you were letting me know what you thought about my chitchat.

B. You are just rude and selfish.

C. I feel like I need to talk because you are so quiet all of the time.

D. _____

14. "You never start conversations. I feel like I am living alone." Your response could be:

A. Guess I feel like I don't have much to say.

B. I feel like I can't get a word in edgewise.

C. You don't seem to listen when I talk.

D. _____

15. "I think you should get a new hairstyle, you look dated." Your response could be:

A. Oh, yeah? When was the last time you looked in the mirror?

B. How dare you be so cruel?

C. Thank you for the suggestion, but I like the style.

D. _____

16. "You make me so mad when you talk to me in that tone." Your response could be:

A. Stop nagging me!

B. I cannot "make you mad." Controlling your emotions is out of my hands.

C. I can't understand what is wrong with that tone. Would you explain?

D. _____

17. "YOU ARE SO SLOPPY! YOUR BELONGINGS ARE scattered all over the place. What are you going to do about it?" Your response could be:

A. Nothing. I am not the one with a problem. You're the neat freak.

B. Jeez, get off my back. You sound like my mother.

C. I didn't know it bothered you so much. I'll try to keep my things out of your way.

D. _____

18. "YOU ARE ON THAT COMPUTER ALL HOURS OF the day and night. You hardly spend any time with me." Your response could be:

A. It's my life, and I can do what I want.

B. I didn't realize that I spend so much time on the computer.

C. I lose track of time when I get on the computer. Let's get out of the house sometime soon and have some fun.

D. _____

19. "YOU ARE ALWAYS AT YOUR PARENT'S HOUSE. When are you going to cut the cord?" Your response could be:

A. You actually sound jealous that I spend time with my family.

B. I think it is important to spend time with my family.

C. Let's take a look at the situation and talk about how to fit in time with my parents within our marriage.

D. _____

20. "YOU ARE TAILGATING AGAIN. I AM WORRIED that we will get into an accident if the car in front of us stops quickly." Your response could be:

A. If you don't like the way I drive, take your own car.

B. Thanks for the reminder.

C. I didn't realize how uncomfortable this makes you. I will drop back now.

D. _____

CHAPTER NINE

COMMUNICATION

"Many marriages would be better if the husband and the wife clearly understood that they are on the same side."

—ZIG ZIGLAR

Before getting married, couples have many opportunities to discuss a variety of issues—everything from the wedding ceremony to more weighty concerns, like what life will be like after the wedding. When couples begin living together (after the wedding or before, if they chose to cohabitate before getting married), they will be in ongoing communication with one another, whether through each other's words in person or via cyberspace, attitudes, facial expressions, body language, physical presence, and/or tone of voice.

Marriage is a 24/7 commitment and the challenge of staying in touch with a partner largely revolves around how well partners communicate with one another. Well-honed communication skills create healthy patterns that can build a strong and vibrant marriage. On the other hand, poor communication skills have been cited as a contributing cause in divorce. Since communication is so important, it may be wise for couples to invest some time looking at their current habits and incorporating more effective communication skills, where needed, into their marriage.

Respect is the number one ingredient in a healthy relationship. If you respect your partner, you will set a positive foundation for all of your communication. People may think, "I love my partner and will always show respect." But sensitive issues will surface, buttons will get pushed, and sarcasm and/or harsh words will probably, at one point or another, turn respect into disrespect.

The examples below demonstrate various ways communication impacts the marriage relationship:

1. YOU HAD AN AWAKENING MOMENT, AND DISCOVERED that you really want to finish your degree program that you left before you met your partner. You:

A. Immediately go to the college and sign up for classes, and do not discuss any time or money issues with your partner.

B. Feel guilty about spending money on yourself and never mention your unfulfilled dream to your partner.

C. Do some research about tuition and scheduling issues and then call a meeting with your partner to share your idea.

D. _____

2. WHILE TALKING TO YOUR PARTNER, YOU NOTICE that his/her attention is elsewhere. You are upset because this is a common occurrence. You feel dissed and:

A. Keep talking and accept that this is the level of attention your partner is capable of.

B. Stop talking. Then let your partner know that it seems he/she is not listening and ask that he/she be more attentive.

C. Accuse him/her of never listening and leave the room.

D. _____

3. THE RENT/MORTGAGE IS DUE ON THE FIRST OF the month. You thought your partner had taken care of sending out the check, while your partner thought you had taken care of this task. A late notice arrives in the mail with a penalty. You:

A. Blame your partner.

B. Wait for your partner to take care of the situation.

C. Suggest you both sit down and clarify how the bills will get paid each month and by whom.

D. _____

4. YOU TELL YOUR PARTNER YOU CAUSED A DENT in the fender of the new car. Your partner turns red and starts yelling at you. You:

A. Yell back.

B. Say you are sorry and will take care of the problem.

C. Request that your partner not yell at you and volunteer to take care of the cost and time to get it fixed.

D. _____

5. YOU WENT OUT TO DINNER WITH A CO-WORKER, who is an ex, and you then felt like this may not have been the right decision. When your partner asks why you were not home for dinner. You:

A. Lie and say you were with a friend.

B. Say, "It is none of your business."

C. Take a deep breath, tell the truth, and apologize for your mistake.

D. _____

6. Your partner asks for a meeting to discuss
household issues. You think these "meetings" are a waste of time. You:

A. Don't show up.

B. Show up for the meeting, turn on the television, and refuse to look your partner in the eye.

C. Show up for the meeting, tell your partner that you are not comfortable in these situations, but are willing to be more open and try to participate.

D. _____

7. You have a big presentation due at work
and your partner calls and wants to chitchat. You:

A. Half listen and hope the conversation ends soon.

B. Let your partner know that you are stressed-out from this work project and say you will call back later.

C. Hang up after the conversation and turn the phone off.

D. _____

8. Your partner has a complaint about you
and uses an offensive tone of voice when telling you. You don't mind getting the feedback about the complaint, but are bothered by the offensive tone. You:

A. Answer your partner in the same tone, which may escalate the negative situation.

B. Calmly, softly, let your partner know that you appreciate him/her letting you know about the issue, but note that it is not acceptable to use that kind of offensive tone.

C. Sarcastically ask if he/she thinks he/she is in a courtroom trying to win a big case.

D. _____

9. YOU MAKE A COMMENT IN JEST THAT YOUR PARTNER
is offended by and he/she grabs your arm. You:

A. Request that he/she let go of your arm and refrain from ever exerting force on you. Then let him/her know that the comment was in jest.

B. Go ahead and grab his/her arm and say, "Thought you'd like to know how this feels!"

C. Say nothing about the inappropriate action and apologize for offending him/her.

D. _____

10. IN A MOMENT OF ANGER, YOU CALL YOUR PARTNER
a horrible name. You immediately know that you have caused potential harm. You:

A. Immediately apologize and explain that in a moment of anger, you did not think before you spoke.

B. Ponder about the situation and decide what you did was justified.

C. Say nothing and hope that your partner did not take offense.

D. _____

CHAPTER TEN:

RESPONSE-ABILITY

The Response Assessment Key at the back of the book determines your response style—Ultimate, Competent, Inconsistent, or Clueless—by tracking your response style preference in specific situations. Simply total the sum of each a, b, and c answer for each chapter. Yet, the real results of this test are what you have learned in this process. Hopefully, you have found something—a particular insight, a hidden strength, or something much more personal—that will help you build a successful marriage through the power of partnership.

Once you have determined the type of partner you are, you can begin to make amends to become the type of partner you want to be.

THE ULTIMATE PARTNER: This partner is willing to collaborate, cooperate, and compromise as well as invest time and energy in taking positive actions that enhance the marriage. This partner is interested in getting things done and will go the extra mile in making sure the marriage is on the right track.

The four distinguishing qualities of the ultimate partner are:

1. He/she is honest and interested in maintaining a sense of clarity in all actions and thoughts.
2. He/she is flexible and open.
3. He/she is encouraging and helpful.
4. He/she is proactive.

Congratulations to you for those times and situations when you are an ultimate partner! Your answers show a deep commitment to the marriage, and illustrate a willingness to talk about issues and be a proactive participant in the relationship.

THE COMPETENT PARTNER: This partner is a positive participant in the marriage overall and is concerned about building a strong partnership in the marriage. This partner demonstrates a willingness to discuss issues, and to take positive actions. There is room for improvement, however. In order for the competent partner to become the ultimate partner, he/she must make an effort to go the extra mile. If a marital issue arises, it is not enough to simply discuss the issue; you must actively do something. Only then will you be able to fully contribute to the marriage.

The four distinguishing qualities of the competent partner are:

1. He/she is open.

2. He/she shows a commitment to discussing marital issues.

3. He/she is cooperative.

4. He/she has a positive attitude.

THE INCONSISTENT PARTNER: This partner is sporadic with his/her reactions. Sometimes he/she is incredibly positive; other times, he/she is highly negative. His/her reactions run the gamut and fluctuate, depending on the circumstance, which may contribute to a cycle of instability in the relationship. Don't fret, though. There is promise and room to grow here. Because some of the options chosen show a willingness to talk, be open, and do what is best for the marriage, there is an opportunity for positive change and growth.

On the down side, some of the inconsistent partner's behavior may be harmful, insulting, or patronizing. The inconsistent partner may take actions that are best for the individual, but not necessarily for the couple. He/she may simply deny or ignore the issue at hand.

The four red flags of inconsistency are:

1. Sometimes the partner is open to talk and truly listens; other times the partner is unwilling to do so.

2. Sometimes there is real honesty; other times there is deceit or denial.

3. Sometimes the partner is treated with utmost respect; other times the partner is treated with disrespect, condescension, and/or sarcasm.

4. Sometimes there is a feeling of intimacy; other times there is an emotional or physical void.

Steps for improvement include adding new behaviors, like those listed under the ultimate partner and the competent partner.

THE CLUELESS PARTNER: This partner, unfortunately, tends to lean toward a general sense of negativity: negative actions, negative words, negative attitude, and an unwillingness to play an active role in building the marriage.

The four distinguishing qualities of the clueless partner are:

1. He/she is resistant to discussing issues.

2. He/she tends to criticize his/her partner.

3. He/she is unwilling to cooperate or compromise.

4. He/she exhibits a desire not to change.

Important Note: Partners may exhibit each of the four styles at different times in their marriage, depending on the situations. The "ultimate" goal is to strive toward responding with respect, love, empathy, openness, and a positive attitude when challenges occur.

CHAPTER ELEVEN

LET'S TALK

*"The goal is to have a conversation in a way so
that you can have another conversation tomorrow."*

—UNKNOWN

There are some basic communication norms in society, like treating others with respect and using a moderate tone of voice when speaking. If you choose to set up some basic communication guidelines at the beginning of your relationship, you will be drawing important boundaries that will stand as the foundation of future discussions, from casual chitchat to more serious disagreements. The simple fact of the matter is that communication problems account for many of the challenges couples face in marriage, and may even contribute to or be the cause of divorce. So, to help you and your partner talk through any number of issues—whether you're planning a vacation, working out a problem, or looking for ideas to show active love—you may use these simple yet effective six marriage communication tools. Refer back to these tools anytime; they're an invaluable resource for helping to create a stable relationship, one based on healthy communication.

Marriage Communication Tool #1:
THE TOP TEN GUIDELINES FOR HEALTHY COMMUNICATION

1. Be respectful. The first and foremost element in healthy communication is that both partners treat each other with respect. When speaking, use a kind tone of voice and look your partner in the eyes. Avoid sarcasm, criticism, and blame.

2. Be a good planner. Decide on the time and place, and the approximate amount of time needed for the discussion. Try to hold important discussions in a neutral area, rather than in the home office, bedroom, or workspace. Honor these agreements.

3. Be prepared. If possible, organize your thoughts beforehand so your intentions are clear.

4. Be present. Avoid making projections about the future, and above all else, do not dredge up unfinished business from the past. Avoid being absentminded and muttering unconvincing "uh-huhs," while thinking about the game/show you are missing or the next task you want to do. Instead, commit to the discussion and keep your mind focused on the task at hand.

5. Be honest. When voicing your concerns, ideas, and opinions, do so with complete honesty.

6. Be a good listener. Listen carefully to everything your partner says and respond with empathy and love.

7. Be positive. Stay away from negative thoughts and comments. Instead, strive for a sense of openness, flexibility, and a willingness to work toward cooperation.

8. Be focused. During discussions, avoid distractions, like watching the television, and keep your complete attention on your partner.

9. Be clear. Reiterate what your partner says to clarify that you're both on same page. Likewise, express yourself in as clear a manner as possible so your partner understands your point of view.

10. More than anything else, be understanding. Try to put yourself in your partner's shoes and see his/her side of the issue, even if his/her perspective is drastically different from yours.

Marriage Communication Tool #2:
DISCUSSION PREP REMINDERS AND MODES

Some questions are easy to answer, like, "What time shall we have dinner?" Other questions, like, "Where are we spending Thanksgiving?" or "How are we going to pay for the expensive car repair?" take more time to figure out and can surface emotional responses.

You and your partner can proceed through life's more complex issues by deciding upon certain conversation protocols. This way, you'll both be on the same page, and you'll know what to expect during discussions.

Every conversation has it own set of goals. Once both of you are aware of the other's goal or "discussion mode," you can orient yourself to the conversation at hand. Mindful that every couple has their own dynamic, the following list of four discussion modes provides a general guide to common conversational elements:

THE FOUR MODES OF DISCUSSION

COLLABORATION: Both partners share thoughts to come to solution.

VENTING: One partner wants to vent and shares information, thoughts, or a story with only one objective: to unload it from his/her mind.

FEEDBACK: One partner wants to share information, thoughts, or a story, and wants feedback on a particular aspect.

INFORMATION GATHERING: One partner needs to get information or needs to ask for help.

Knowing what mode you're in helps clear the intentions for any conversation. If an issue goes unresolved, set up a follow-up meeting. If the issue is still unresolved after a second discussion, you and your partner may have hit a slight roadblock, in which case Marriage Communication Tool #3: Strategies for Roadblocks, may be especially helpful.

Communication Reminders

1. BEFORE STARTING A DISCUSSION, TAKE FIVE SECONDS AND remind yourself of the unconditional love you feel for your partner and of your commitment to act in a respectable manner.

2. ACTIONS SPEAK LOUDER THAN WORDS. SO, REMEMBER: Bored looks and folded arms may give signals that you are not open or interested in what your partner has to say.

3. YOUR TONE OF VOICE CAN RANGE FROM A WHISPER TO A scream. Choose a friendly, respectful tone. Avoid harsh tones, which can be offensive.

4. LOOK INTO YOUR PARTNER'S EYES. IF YOU SHIFT YOUR EYES all over the room or stare at the floor, it may appear that you are trying to avoid your partner or aren't interested in what he/she says.

5. YOU ARE BOTH ONLY HUMAN AND MAKE MISTAKES. LEARN TO accept and forgive the small stuff and keep in mind that, as individuals, you will sometimes have different opinions and behaviors from one another.

6. TREAT YOUR PARTNER AS YOU WOULD LIKE TO BE TREATED.

7. THINK BEFORE YOU SAY ANYTHING! OTHERWISE, YOU MAY find your foot in your mouth, wishing you could take back some thing you said.

8. THE SECRET TO OPENING THE DOOR TO AGREEMENT, collaboration, and/or cooperation is to maintain a sense of openness to whatever your partner tells you. Only then will you be able to understand each other's point of view.

9. EVEN IF YOU UNDERSTAND WHERE YOUR PARTNER IS coming from, remember that you do not have the power to change his/her mind, no matter how badly you may want to. Instead, respect your partner and work toward accepting—while not necessarily agreeing with—his/her viewpoint.

10. AVOID BLAME. IT'S NOT CONSTRUCTIVE AND ITS NEGATIVITY is damaging and not worth the consequences.

11. LISTEN, REALLY LISTEN, AND THEN REVIEW WHAT YOUR partner has said and rephrase the information, asking, "Do I understand what you said . . . ?"

Marriage Communication Tool #3:
STRATEGIES FOR ROADBLOCKS

When two people disagree and both refuse to budge, they are at a stalemate or a roadblock. They can then try a new strategy and hope that they can work things out. One of the best methods, or starting points, for shifting strategies is to gain a new perspective. To do this, first objectively reiterate or review whatever is already known about the problematic situation. Listen to your partner with an open mind and without any judgment about where he/she is coming from. A perspective shift may occur when there is more clarity about the situation. For example, when a partner reiterates how important a particular issue is to him/her, the other partner may recognize that the request for change is heartfelt and he/she may be more willing to compromise. If this strategy fails, gather more information on the subject, if possible. Whether the problem has to do with money, work, family, the household, or the relationship itself, spending time to get more information won't hurt, and it might help.

Once more information has been gathered, create a pro/con list. Since it is difficult to recall everything said in discussions, listing your ideas in a pro and con format allows both of you to clearly see both sides of an issue. After doing this exercise, the answer may be clear. Even if there is no resolution to the problem, you will both have had the chance to state your views in written form and read what is on your partner's mind.

When no solution is in sight, brainstorm other possible solutions, writing down your suggestions on paper. Follow the simple guideline that whatever you or your partner says will not be judged. Think outside of the box and let your creativity guide you toward a common ground for cooperation or compromise. Who knows? Maybe one of you might change your opinion in the spirit of cooperation. Or, maybe one of the ideas will be outside of the box and bring you both to agreement.

If none of the above works, try asking the question, "How important is this?" or "What will this matter a year from now?" Your answer may reveal that the issue really isn't that big of a deal and is not worth the time and emotional energy of arguing.

During this process, it is possible that one of you may give in to the other purely out of weakness, exhaustion, or fear. While this may be done in the spirit of playing the role of "peacemaker," it is not a helpful solution—for either one of you. If repeated regularly, the "peacemaker" may not only lose a voice in the decision-making process, he/she may also never learn to stand firm on his/her beliefs. This doesn't benefit the other person, either. A healthy relationship is one built on strength and honesty. It is only as strong as the sum of its two parts; if one person comes from a place of weakness, the entire relationship suffers.

In some unfortunate circumstances, there may not be a solution to the problem. If you've exhausted every strategy and can't see a turning point, you have three remaining options: 1) Give up and carry a resentment; 2) Continue to try to change the situation, perhaps seeking professional counsel; 3) Accept the situation as it is. While option number three sounds just as healthy as option number two, there are instances when acceptance can be just as damaging as option number one. If you are in an abusive relationship, for example, and/or if safety is an issue, there are resources available to help you. An abusive relationship, whether it's emotionally, verbally, or physically threatening, is one roadblock that may require professional help. In less serious situations, however, it's likely that you and your partner will reach a mutually beneficial understanding if you proceed with love and respect for one another's viewpoints.

Marriage Communication Tool #4: THE WEEKLY MEETING

Though this concept may seem formal and unromantic, it is a tool that can reap plentiful benefits. The weekly meeting gives you and your partner a simple yet effective way to keep connected on a regular basis. Schedule one hour or even half of an hour per week to compare notes on each partner's activities, plans, social happenings, and/or household responsibilities. Daily e-mail updates and phone exchanges help couples stay connected, but there is nothing like a face-to-face discussion. Sharing work schedules and appointments not only helps you determine what times will be free for meals and shared activities, it also guarantees that you won't have scheduling conflicts. During these weekly meetings, refer to this quick list of helpful tips to make sure you're both up-to-the-minute with each other's calendar and responsibilities:

• Review the calendar for upcoming social activities, birthdays, anniversaries, holidays, and make sure that there is something fun planned for that particular day.

• Review the weekly bills and your financial status. Are there bills that need to be paid soon? If so, make a plan of how this task will get done. During your meeting, take the time, too, to discuss larger financial goals, like possible investments and vacation funds.

• Review the weekly household chores, and make sure responsibilities for each task are discussed and divvied up.

• Check in with one another on specific issues that may be affecting your calendar, like, "How can we spend more time together?; How can we have more fun?; or, How can we bring more friends into our lives?" The answers to these questions will inevitably depend on how you plan more activities into your day-to-day routine.

• Use the weekly meeting as an opportunity to plan a discussion for a more serious issue that needs to come to light.

If you miss one of your weekly meetings, don't fret. Just be sure to make the next one so you don't create a pattern of neglect. The more on top of the meetings that you are, the better chance you'll have of creating healthy communication in your marriage.

Marriage Communication Tool #5:
MARRIAGE MANTRAS

What costs nothing, takes a few seconds to do, and has the potential to change a negative attitude to a positive one, open the door to forgiveness, and serve as a reminder that we can't change the other person and that no one is perfect? Answer: a marriage mantra.

A marriage mantra is a short phrase or sentence(s) that serves as a helpful reminder of our original intentions with respect to marriage. A marriage mantra has the added benefit of replacing negative thoughts with positive, informative ones. When negative thoughts and feelings cloud your perspective, it's easy to get stuck in a rut of frustration. Taking a few seconds to repeat positive statements like these listed here may have a calming effect on you and may actually help to change your perspective. If your marital situation gets difficult, take a deep breath and repeat these mantras:

"I cannot change the other person, but I can change my own attitude."

"I cannot read another person's mind, and no one can read my mind."

"No one is perfect."

"At any point of the day, I can begin again."

These mantras can be very helpful, especially in the midst of a heated discussion. Use the space below to write down your own marriage mantras.

_____

_____

_____

_____

_____

_____

_____

_____

_____

_____

_____

Marriage Communication Tool #6: The Summit

An Annual Retreat to Reconnect and Celebrate Marriage

An annual retreat weekend or vacation is an opportunity to reconnect on a romantic level, review, and celebrate positive aspects of the prior year as well as plan for the year ahead. Taking a romantic weekend can do wonders for a marriage, giving partners a bit of relaxation and creating an opportunity to "fall in love" all over again. The cost for staying in a hotel and going out for meals can be the best investment a couple can make for the sake of their marriage and their relationship.

The retreat need not be extravagant. If planned properly, you can host a retreat within your own home! Instead of going out for a fancy dinner, cook a nice meal together and give the dining room the five-star treatment: candles, tablecloth, flowers, and chilled champagne. Instead of going to a spa for a massage, try your hand at couples massage or prepare a nice bath for your loved one. Sometimes staying in can be just as relaxing as taking that big vacation.

But there seems to be re-creational magic in "just getting away," if only for an overnight.

Chapter Twelve:
TAKING CARE OF THE SELF

It is important that you take care of yourself and love yourself before you try to take care of and love others. The basics of self-care are simple. Eat nutritious food. Get enough rest. Exercise. Show responsible behavior. Enjoy your interests. Stay connected to friends and family. Though basic self-care is a simple concept, it is not easy to practice. The reality is that to take care of one's physical, mental, emotional, spiritual, and social aspects requires time, planning, and energy. People's busy schedules don't seem to allow the time to make significant changes, especially concerning exercise and/or diet.

It is very common for one partner to overextend his/her own time and energy to take care of his/her partner and neglect their own care of self. This may work for a while. Over time, though, this pattern may prove to be draining to the caretaker and have a negative effect on his/her health and on the marriage relationship and cause codependence. This kind of negative relationship might be avoided if partners have a clear sense of identity. One way to get a sense of self-appraisal is to ask questions, such as: "Who am I?" and "What do I want out of life?" Taking the time to clarify your goals, dreams, and desires prepares you to answer questions with your own thoughts rather than the old stand-bys, like, "I don't know," "I can't decide," "It is up to you." Answers like these promote unhealthy patterns of: 1) not knowing what your real desires are; 2) leaving important decisions to someone else; 3) avoiding any real sense of personal responsibility; and 4) spending time in a perpetual state of indecision.

The goals of the following exercises are to help you create an image in your mind of who you want to be, what you want to do in life, and how you can make steps to achieve these goals. These exercises can create a clearer picture of yourself and your goals so that when you begin to build your marriage, you can clearly let your partner know your dreams for yourself and for your marriage. The following exercise can help you identify your interests and motivate you to take the actions you would like to take, both in your marriage and in life.

Exercise One: ACTIVITIES INVENTORY AND WISH LIST

To develop into the individual one dreams of becoming requires first taking a personal inventory of one's life activities and then making a wish list of activities to incorporate into one's life plan. Note: This exercise requires a pen, a blank sheet of paper, twenty minutes, and some imagination.

Begin by folding the paper into four columns and write one header on each: past activities, present activities, future activities, and activities in marriage.

Take five minutes to quickly write a list of activities you enjoyed as a child and in the past. Envision yourself experiencing these moments.

Take five minutes to write a list of activities that you love to do on a regular basis now.

Review these lists and let your imagination run wild for five minutes to write a list of activities you would like to do in the future.

Next, look at all of these wonderful activities you have enjoyed and/or plan to enjoy, and make a list of the activities that you would like to include in your marriage.

These lists can serve as a reference to help create the kind of life you want to live and the kind of marriage you want to share.

Exercise Two: BUILDING A COLLAGE

This exercise requires an openness and willingness to use your imagination to make a collage of what you would like your life and marriage to look like. If you'd like to, invite your partner to do this exercise, too.

Don't Forget: THE A,B,Cs OF SELF-CARE

SOMETIMES WE GET SO BUSY WE TEND TO FORGET THE BASICS— the A, B, Cs of life. Here are some helpful self-nurturing reminders to keep life in perspective:

A: Actions and attitude are up to you.
B: Be prepared and be in the moment.
C: Care for yourself and others.
D: Dare to take healthy risks.
E: Eat healthy foods.
F: Forgive, have faith, and have fun.
G: Give away gifts.
H: Humor. Find it in yourself and with others.
I: Initiate your dreams.
J: Journal daily.
K: Know thyself.
L: Love.
M: Meditate.
N: Negotiate with justice.
O: Open your heart and mind.
P: Plan.
Q: Quit complaining.
R: Rest.
S: Smile.
T: Think before you act.
U: Understand, rather than be understood.
V: Visit others.
W: Walk tall.
X: X-ercise.
Y: You. Always take care of you.
Z: Zest. You only go around once, so live your life with zest.

Take a pile of magazines, a piece of poster board, scissors, tape, and markers, and tear or cut appealing images. Then decorate the board with your ideas and favorite images of romantic settings, food, vacation, responsibilities, work, fun activities, photos, et cetera. Consider this collage a reflection of how you envision your marriage and future to be.

Just have fun choosing images, photos, illustrations, and words that reflect your dreams and visions of what you would like your life and your marriage to look like. These images will be reminders of what you desire.

Set the collage aside or store it somewhere special so you can check back occasionally to see if your dreams and goals turn into realities.

Invite your partner to also create a collage. If he/she does not do the exercise, you can still share your creation and let him/her know what you are thinking and dreaming about your future together.

Exercise Three: VISUALIZE YOUR FUTURE

The goal of this exercise is to imagine what your future will be like at different points in time. The process of visualizing what life will be like a year from now or ten years from now can provide a glimpse into your dreams and desires. If time is invested in this kind of daydream, the images may even become a reality. So, get comfortable, relax and visualize what you will be doing and what your life and marriage will be like in:

1 Year
5 Years
10 Years
20 Years

Jot down your thoughts about each time frame for future reference. There may be clues about where you want to live, family plans, vacations, and job situations. You may use this exercise often to clarify your dreams and set new goals. If you already have a general idea of what you desire, chances are good that you can use this exercise to help make make plans and choices that will create the life and marriage of your dreams.

Balancing Act

HERE ARE SOME HELPFUL, QUICK REMINDERS for those of you who are faced with one or more issues at hand:

1. Appreciate the love. Remind yourself how lucky you are that out of all the people on earth your partner chose you.

2. Think first before you speak. Get the issue clear in your mind first so you can communicate exactly what you are thinking.

3. Respect your partner. When discussing issues, always treat your partner as you would like to be treated.

4. Commit to investing time. Accept that sharing the joys of marriage and working out issues takes time and energy.

5. Brainstorm for options. The higher number of options may provide the best chance for collaboration.

6. Stay cool. Try to stay calm during discussions. Taking a deep breath now and then might help.

7. Use "I" statements. Owning opinions and emotions is a responsible way of communicating and avoids blame.

8. Stay focused. Stay on the topic; do not avoid the issue.

9. Pick your battles. Some issues are worth spending a lot of time and energy on, and some are just not worth the effort.

10. Partnership power. Last but not least, remember that marriage offers the opportunity for two people to share all aspects of life together, giving them partnership power that they can use to build a beautiful marriage, life, and family, and help each other make their individual dreams come true.

Chapter Thirteen:
A Parting Gift

"Grow old along with me. The best is yet to be
—the last of life for which the first was made."

—Robert Browning

As noted earlier, marriage is created by the many decisions made on a daily basis by each partner in the relationship. It is my wish that readers will make choices that will help create the marriage of their dreams. Hopefully there was information in the *PMAT* that may be of help to you and your partner at some time. Please keep in mind that this book can be used as a reference whenever new challenges occur.

Last but not least, I'd like to share some thoughts on love. Marriage is made up of a variety of loves. There is the initial "falling-in-love" love and, later, a combination of other types of loves: unconditional love, friendship love, sensual love, romantic love, and every shade in between. Love is the thread that keeps the marriage alive.

Thoughts of love are sweet, but if left unspoken, cannot be shared or communicated.

Words of love are beautiful, as expressed in poetry, songs, and caring phrases. But words alone are sometimes meaningless without action. Since actions do speak louder than words, here is a "gift" list of suggestions and reminders for couples to actively show love, help nurture and/or improve the relationship, and help keep their marriage on an even keel.

To those readers planning a wedding: May the love, joy, and happiness you experience on your wedding day continue throughout your marriage. To those readers already married: May you remember why you made the choice to share your life with the other person and may you continue to work together to keep a bond of love, respect, and support.

One Hundred Ways to Show Active Love

1. Take care of your partner during an illness.

2. Pick up your partner when he/she falls.

3. Forgive your partner for his/her mistakes.

4. Love your partner, even on bad-hair days.

5. Burst with pride at your partner's accomplishments.

6. Give a smile when your partner is down.

7. Give extra-special hugs on his/her stressful days.

8. Walk arm in arm while shopping.

9. Fix his/her favorite meal.

10. Serve him/her chicken soup in times of the flu.

11. Give your partner a gift (like a favorite CD) he/she wanted.

12. Give your partner a ride home from the dentist after a painful root canal.

13. Do a favor for your exhausted partner.

14. Give your partner a pass for the occasional loss of temper.

15. Share the burdens of the world.

16. Share the cost of living.

17. Pool your resources for a special event.

18. Notice and share his/her joy, happiness, and enthusiasm.

19. Give your partner a hug when he/she is sad.

20. Tell your partner when there is spinach stuck between his/her teeth.

21. Make love passionately.

22. Make love in a beautiful way.

23. Leave a chocolate treat on your partner's pillow.

24. Send caring messages via e-mail. (But carefully avoid abusing work Internet guidelines.)

25. Take your partner to concerts.

26. Walk with your partner and enjoy nature.

27. Offer to help put the groceries away.

28. Hold your partner when he/she is worried.

29. Accept your partners choice of clothes.

30. Leave "I love you" voice mail messages.

31. Listen, really listen, to what your partner says.

32. Share your enthusiasm about your partner's new ideas.

33. Stay with your partner through thick and thin.

34. Offer to rent and watch a favorite movie.

35. Offer to help edit and/or write résumés and/or cover letters.

36. Hold your partner's hand during scary times, like chemotherapy.

37. Always remember your partner's birthday.

38. Leave surprise notes on your partner's pillow.

39. Send special greeting cards randomly.

40. Spend extra energy to find a special way to say "happy anniversary."

41. When you make a mistake, apologize.

42. Show love often.

43. Remember to call when coming home late.

44. Be willing to sometimes let go of an argument.

45. When you see your partner at his/her worst, love him/her anyway.

46. Offer your willingness to cooperate.

47. Give your partner massages.

48. Gaze at your partner with loving eyes.

49. Wink from across the room to show that you care.

50. Look on the bright side of life.

51. Wear the special gift your partner has given to you.

52. Share your hopes and dreams.

53. Vent when you feel the need.

54. Share memories together.

55. Take your partner on a date to a bookstore.

56. Wash the car for your partner.

57. Light lots of candles and be romantic often.

58. Draw your partner a hot, relaxing bath.

59. Play a favorite slow song, and request a dance.

60. Tell your partner how attractive he/she is.

61. Say marriage makes your life feel full.

62. Offer to drive.

63. Teach your partner your expert grilling skills.

64. Plan a surprise birthday celebration.

65. Say, "You are the only one for me!"

66. Love, accept, and support your partner.

67. Discuss issues, concerns, dreams, and fears regularly.

68. Show love through actions each day.

69. Share the responsibilities of marriage and the home.

70. Say "thank you" often.

71. Communicate clearly and honestly always.

72. Show respect consistently.

73. Share goals of marriage and life.

74. Make intimacy a priority in and out of the bedroom, day after day.

75. Remind each other of your marriage commitment.

76. Be empathetic.

77. Give compliments.

78. Have a special date at least once a week.

79. Practice gratitude.

80. Keep a gratitude journal.

81. Accept that we are human and make mistakes.

82. Practice trust.

83. Compromise once in a while.

84. State that no two people are alike, or think alike in times of conflict.

85. Ask for clarification because you cannot read your partner's mind.

86. Communicate clearly because your partner cannot read your mind.

87. Speak tenderly.

88. Voice your expectations.

89. Say, "I love you" in the morning.

90. Say, "I love you" before going to sleep.

91. Never go to bed angry at your partner.

92. Smile often at your partner.

93. Write important dates on the calendar.

94. Have a weekly meeting to share information and keep in touch.

95. Have a to-do list to help get tasks done and stay more organized.

96. Keep family and home information in one central place.

97. Have fun.

98. Don't take your partner for granted!

99. Change your attitude, when needed.

100. Remind yourself and your partner that marriage is what you and your partner make it.

Resources

Issues and conflicts will arise in a marriage, and partners usually work though challenges and conflicts on their own. There will probably come a time when there is a need or a desire to reach out for help. Partners may just want more information about sex or how to get closer as a couple. Or, there may be serious issues that involve abuse, threats, or dangerous situations. In those cases, it is advisable for both partners, if possible, to seek the professional help of a counselor or clergyperson, or if necessary, social services or law enforcement.

Below are examples of resources that range from books with more comprehensive advice than offered here to professional organizations that deal with marriage issues.

Books on Marriage Preparation and Maintenance

Bloom, Linda, and Charlie Bloom. *101 Things I Wish I Knew When I Got Married: Simple Lessons to Make Love Last.* New World Library, 2004.

Glasser, William, and Carleen Glasser. *Eight Lessons for a Happier Marriage.* Harper, 2007.

Gottman, Julie Schwartz, John M. Gottman and Joan De Claire, *10 Lessons to Transform Your Marriage: Case Studies and Advice from the Nation's Premier Relationship Experts.* Random House, 2006.

McMickel, Marvin A. *Before We Say I Do: 7 Steps to a Healthy Marriage.* Judson Press, 2003.

Parrott, Leslie, and Les Parrott. *Saving Your Marriage Before It Starts: Seven Questions to Ask Before (and After) You Marry.* Zondervan, 1995.

Books on Personal Growth

Byrne, Rhonda. *The Secret.* Atria/Beyond Words, 2006.

Cameron, Julia. *The Artist's Way: A Spiritual Path to Higher Creativity.* Tarcher/Putnam, 1992.

Dyer, Wayne W. *The Power of Intention: Learning to Co-Create Your World Your Way.* Hay House, 2004.

———. *Your Erroneous Zones: Escape Negative Thinking and Take Control of Your Life.* Funk & Wagnalls, 1976.

Professional Counseling Organizations

American Association for Marriage and Family Therapy
112 South Alfred Street, Alexandria, VA 22314-3061
http://www.aamft.org
Telephone: 703-838-9808

American Counseling Association
5999 Stevenson Avenue, Alexandria, VA 22304
Telephone: 800-347-6647
TDD/TTY: 703-823-6862
http://www.counseling.org

American Psychological Association
750 First Street NE, Washington, DC 20002-4242
http://www.APAHelpCenter.org
Telephone: 800-374-2721
TDD/TTY: 202-336-6123

National Institute of Mental Health
6001 Executive Boulevard, Room 8184, MSC 9663
Bethesda, MD 20892-9663
http://www.nimh.nih.gov/
Telephone: 866-615-6464
TDD/TTY: 866-415-8051

Marriage Programs/Seminars

The Marriage Builders
12568 Ethan Avenue North
White Bear Lake, MN 55110
http://www.MarriageBuilders.com
Telephone: 651-762-8570

Relationship Seminars, Inc.
7750 N. MacArthur, Suite 120-241
Irving, TX 75063
http://www.RelationshipRich.org
Telephone: 888-293-7790

Worldwide Marriage Encounter, Inc.
2210 East Highland Avenue, Suite 106
San Bernardino, CA 92404-4666
http://www.wwme.org
Telephone: 909-863-9963

Online Marriage Information

MarriageAdvice.com
4815 FM 2351, Suite 201
Friendswood, TX 77546
http://www.MarriageAdvice.com
Telephone: 281-993-5657

Smart Marriages: The Coalition for Marriage, Family and Couples Education
5310 Belt Rd NW
Washington, DC 20015
http://www.SmartMarriages.com
Telephone: 202-362-3332

RESPONSE SHEET Circle one response answer per question. Note that to get the most accurate response-assessment score, the answers should be A, B, or C.

CHAPTER TWO: HOME AND HARMONY	CHAPTER THREE: FOOD, FITNESS, AND HEALTH	CHAPTER FOUR: TOGETHERNESS
1. a b c d	1. a b c d	1. a b c d
2. a b c d	2. a b c d	2. a b c d
3. a b c d	3. a b c d	3. a b c d
4. a b c d	4. a b c d	4. a b c d
5. a b c d	5. a b c d	5. a b c d
6. a b c d	6. a b c d	6. a b c d
7. a b c d	7. a b c d	7. a b c d
8. a b c d	8. a b c d	8. a b c d
9. a b c d	9. a b c d	9. a b c d
10. a b c d	10. a b c d	10. a b c d
11. a b c d	11. a b c d	11. a b c d
12. a b c d	12. a b c d	12. a b c d
13. a b c d	13. a b c d	13. a b c d
14. a b c d	14. a b c d	14. a b c d
15. a b c d	15. a b c d	15. a b c d
16. a b c d	16. a b c d	16. a b c d
17. a b c d	17. a b c d	17. a b c d
18. a b c d	18. a b c d	18. a b c d
19. a b c d	19. a b c d	19. a b c d
20. a b c d	20. a b c d	20. a b c d
21. a b c d	21. a b c d	21. a b c d
22. a b c d	22. a b c d	22. a b c d
23. a b c d	23. a b c d	23. a b c d
24. a b c d	24. a b c d	24. a b c d
25. a b c d	25. a b c d	25. a b c d
26. a b c d	26. a b c d	26. a b c d
27. a b c d	27. a b c d	27. a b c d
28. a b c d	28. a b c d	28. a b c d
29. a b c d	29. a b c d	29. a b c d
	30. a b c d	30. a b c d
	31. a b c d	31. a b c d

32. a b c d
33. a b c d
34. a b c d
35. a b c d
36. a b c d
37. a b c d

CHAPTER FIVE: FAMILY AND FRIENDS

1. a b c d
2. a b c d
3. a b c d
4. a b c d
5. a b c d
6. a b c d
7. a b c d
8. a b c d
9. a b c d
10. a b c d
11. a b c d
12. a b c d
13. a b c d
14. a b c d
15. a b c d
16. a b c d
17. a b c d
18. a b c d
19. a b c d
20. a b c d
21. a b c d
22. a b c d
23. a b c d

CHAPTER SIX: BALANCING SEX, INTIMACY, AND PERSONAL BOUNDARIES

1. a b c d
2. a b c d
3. a b c d
4. a b c d
5. a b c d
6. a b c d
7. a b c d

8. a b c d
9. a b c d
10. a b c d
11. a b c d
12. a b c d
13. a b c d
14. a b c d
15. a b c d
16. a b c d
17. a b c d
18. a b c d
19. a b c d
20. a b c d
21. a b c d
22. a b c d
23. a b c d
24. a b c d
25. a b c d
26. a b c d

CHAPTER SEVEN: MONEY, MONEY, MONEY

1. a b c d
2. a b c d
3. a b c d
4. a b c d
5. a b c d
6. a b c d
7. a b c d
8. a b c d
9. a b c d
10. a b c d
11. a b c d
12. a b c d
13. a b c d
14. a b c d
15. a b c d
16. a b c d
17. a b c d
18. a b c d
19. a b c d
20. a b c d

21. a b c d
22. a b c d
23. a b c d
24. a b c d

CHAPTER EIGHT: HELPFUL HINTS OR ATTACKS?

1. a b c d
2. a b c d
3. a b c d
4. a b c d
5. a b c d
6. a b c d
7. a b c d
8. a b c d
9. a b c d
10. a b c d
11. a b c d
12. a b c d
13. a b c d
14. a b c d
15. a b c d
16. a b c d
17. a b c d
18. a b c d
19. a b c d
20. a b c d

CHAPTER NINE: COMMUNICATION

1. a b c d
2. a b c d
3. a b c d
4. a b c d
5. a b c d
6. a b c d
7. a b c d
8. a b c d
9. a b c d
10. a b c d

RESPONSE SHEET Circle one response answer per question. Note that to get the most accurate response-assessment score, the answers should be A, B, or C.

CHAPTER TWO: HOME AND HARMONY	CHAPTER THREE: FOOD, FITNESS, AND HEALTH	CHAPTER FOUR: TOGETHERNESS
1. a b c d	1. a b c d	1. a b c d
2. a b c d	2. a b c d	2. a b c d
3. a b c d	3. a b c d	3. a b c d
4. a b c d	4. a b c d	4. a b c d
5. a b c d	5. a b c d	5. a b c d
6. a b c d	6. a b c d	6. a b c d
7. a b c d	7. a b c d	7. a b c d
8. a b c d	8. a b c d	8. a b c d
9. a b c d	9. a b c d	9. a b c d
10. a b c d	10. a b c d	10. a b c d
11. a b c d	11. a b c d	11. a b c d
12. a b c d	12. a b c d	12. a b c d
13. a b c d	13. a b c d	13. a b c d
14. a b c d	14. a b c d	14. a b c d
15. a b c d	15. a b c d	15. a b c d
16. a b c d	16. a b c d	16. a b c d
17. a b c d	17. a b c d	17. a b c d
18. a b c d	18. a b c d	18. a b c d
19. a b c d	19. a b c d	19. a b c d
20. a b c d	20. a b c d	20. a b c d
21. a b c d	21. a b c d	21. a b c d
22. a b c d	22. a b c d	22. a b c d
23. a b c d	23. a b c d	23. a b c d
24. a b c d	24. a b c d	24. a b c d
25. a b c d	25. a b c d	25. a b c d
26. a b c d	26. a b c d	26. a b c d
27. a b c d	27. a b c d	27. a b c d
28. a b c d	28. a b c d	28. a b c d
29. a b c d	29. a b c d	29. a b c d
	30. a b c d	30. a b c d
	31. a b c d	31. a b c d

32. a b c d
33. a b c d
34. a b c d
35. a b c d
36. a b c d
37. a b c d

CHAPTER FIVE: FAMILY AND FRIENDS

1. a b c d
2. a b c d
3. a b c d
4. a b c d
5. a b c d
6. a b c d
7. a b c d
8. a b c d
9. a b c d
10. a b c d
11. a b c d
12. a b c d
13. a b c d
14. a b c d
15. a b c d
16. a b c d
17. a b c d
18. a b c d
19. a b c d
20. a b c d
21. a b c d
22. a b c d
23. a b c d

CHAPTER SIX: BALANCING SEX, INTIMACY, AND PERSONAL BOUNDARIES

1. a b c d
2. a b c d
3. a b c d
4. a b c d
5. a b c d
6. a b c d
7. a b c d

8. a b c d
9. a b c d
10. a b c d
11. a b c d
12. a b c d
13. a b c d
14. a b c d
15. a b c d
16. a b c d
17. a b c d
18. a b c d
19. a b c d
20. a b c d
21. a b c d
22. a b c d
23. a b c d
24. a b c d
25. a b c d
26. a b c d

CHAPTER SEVEN: MONEY, MONEY, MONEY

1. a b c d
2. a b c d
3. a b c d
4. a b c d
5. a b c d
6. a b c d
7. a b c d
8. a b c d
9. a b c d
10. a b c d
11. a b c d
12. a b c d
13. a b c d
14. a b c d
15. a b c d
16. a b c d
17. a b c d
18. a b c d
19. a b c d
20. a b c d

21. a b c d
22. a b c d
23. a b c d
24. a b c d

CHAPTER EIGHT: HELPFUL HINTS OR ATTACKS?

1. a b c d
2. a b c d
3. a b c d
4. a b c d
5. a b c d
6. a b c d
7. a b c d
8. a b c d
9. a b c d
10. a b c d
11. a b c d
12. a b c d
13. a b c d
14. a b c d
15. a b c d
16. a b c d
17. a b c d
18. a b c d
19. a b c d
20. a b c d

CHAPTER NINE: COMMUNICATION

1. a b c d
2. a b c d
3. a b c d
4. a b c d
5. a b c d
6. a b c d
7. a b c d
8. a b c d
9. a b c d
10. a b c d

Response Assessment Key

CHAPTER TWO: HOME AND HARMONY

	A	B	C	D
1.	-5	-10	5	0
2.	5	-5	-10	0
3.	-10	-5	5	0
4.	0	5	-10	0
5.	5	-5	10	0
6.	-5	5	5	0
7.	0	5	10	0
8.	-5	5	5	0
9.	5	5	-10	0
10.	-10	-5	10	0
11.	5	0	-5	0
12.	5	0	-5	0
13.	-5	-5	5	0
14.	5	-5	10	0
15.	5	0	-5	0
16.	10	5	-5	0
17.	-5	-5	10	0
18.	-5	-5	10	0
19.	5	5	-5	0
20.	-5	5	-5	0
21.	-5	5	0	0
22.	-5	10	-5	0
23.	-10	5	5	0
24.	-5	-5	5	0
25.	-5	5	-5	0
26.	5	5	-5	0
27.	-5	5	5	0
28.	-5	10	-5	0
29.	-5	5	0	0

TOTAL _____

Ultimate 100 TO 109
Competent 0 TO 95
Inconsistent -5 TO -95
Clueless -100 TO -175

CHAPTER THREE: FOOD, FITNESS, AND HEALTH

	A	B	C	D
1.	-5	-5	5	0
2.	5	-5	5	0
3.	-10	5	-5	0
4.	10	-10	-5	0
5.	-5	5	-5	0
6.	-5	0	5	0
7.	-5	-10	5	0
8.	-10	5	0	0
9.	-5	5	5	0
10.	5	5	-5	0
11.	-5	-5	5	0
12.	-5	10	5	0
13.	-5	-5	5	0
14.	-5	10	5	0
15.	5	5	-5	0
16.	5	-5	10	0
17.	5	-5	-5	0
18.	5	5	-5	0
19.	5	-5	-5	0
20.	-5	-10	5	0
21.	-5	5	5	0
22.	5	-5	-5	0
23.	5	-5	-5	0
24.	-5	5	10	0
25.	5	-5	10	0
26.	5	5	-5	0
27.	5	-5	5	0
28.	-5	5	10	0
29.	0	-5	5	0
30.	5	5	-5	0
31.	5	5	-5	0

TOTAL _____

Ultimate 100 TO 190
Competent 0 TO 95
Inconsistent -5 TO -95
Clueless -100 TO -180

CHAPTER FOUR: TOGETHERNESS

	A	B	C	D
1.	5	-5	-10	0
2.	-10	5	-5	0
3.	-10	5	5	0
4.	-5	5	0	0
5.	-5	-5	5	0
6.	-5	-5	5	0
7.	-5	5	-5	0
8.	5	5	-5	0
9.	5	5	0	0
10.	5	5	-5	0
11.	5	-5	5	0
12.	5	-5	-5	0
13.	-5	-5	5	0
14.	5	5	5	0
15.	-5	5	5	0
16.	10	-5	-5	0
17.	-5	5	5	0
18.	0	-5	5	0
19.	-5	-10	5	0
20.	-5	5	-5	0
21.	5	-5	-5	0
22.	5	-5	5	0
23.	5	-5	5	0
24.	-5	-5	5	0
25.	-5	5	-5	0
26.	5	-5	5	0
27.	5	0	-5	0
28.	5	-5	0	0
29.	5	-5	5	0
30.	10	-5	-5	0
31.	5	-10	-5	0
32.	5	5	-5	0
33.	-5	-10	5	0
34.	5	-5	-10	0
35.	5	-5	-5	0
36.	5	-5	-5	0
37.	-5	5	-10	0

TOTAL _____

Ultimate 100 TO 210
Competent 0 TO 90
Inconsistent -5 TO -120
Clueless -125 TO -245

CHAPTER FIVE: FAMILY AND FRIENDS

	A	B	C	D
1.	5	5	-5	0
2.	-5	5	-5	0
3.	0	5	-10	0
4.	5	0	-5	0
5.	5	-5	5	0
6.	5	-5	5	0
7.	-5	5	5	0
8.	-5	5	5	0
9.	5	-5	5	0
10.	5	-5	-5	0
11.	-5	-10	5	0
12.	5	-5	10	0
13.	-5	-10	5	0
14.	-5	-5	5	0
15.	0	-5	5	0
16.	-5	5	5	0
17.	-5	5	5	0

	A	B	C	D
18.	-5	5	-5	O
19.	-5	5	O	O
20.	-5	5	O	O
21.	5	5	-5	O
22.	5	-5	-5	O
23.	-5	5	-5	O

TOTAL _____

ULTIMATE 65 TO 120
COMPETENT 0 TO 60
INCONSISTENT -5 TO -65
CLUELESS -70 TO -130

CHAPTER SIX: BALANCING SEX, INTIMACY, AND PERSONAL BOUNDARIES

	A	B	C	D
1.	O	5	-5	O
2.	-5	5	-5	O
3.	-5	-5	5	O
4.	-5	5	-5	O
5.	-5	-10	10	O
6.	5	-5	5	O
7.	-5	-5	10	O
8.	5	10	-5	O
9.	-5	5	10	O
10.	-5	5	5	O
11.	O	-5	5	O
12.	-5	-5	5	O
13.	5	-5	-5	O
14.	5	5	-5	O
15.	5	5	-5	O
16.	-5	5	5	O
17.	5	O	-5	O
18.	5	-5	5	O
19.	5	5	-5	O
20.	5	-5	-5	O
21.	5	5	-5	O
22.	-5	-5	5	O
23.	-5	5	5	O
24.	-5	5	5	O
25.	-10	5	-5	O
26.	-5	5	-10	O

TOTAL _____

ULTIMATE 75 TO 150
COMPETENT 0 TO 70
INCONSISTENT -5 TO -70
CLUELESS -75 TO -145

CHAPTER SEVEN: MONEY, MONEY, MONEY

	A	B	C	D
1.	-5	5	-5	O
2.	5	O	-5	O
3.	-10	5	-5	O
4.	5	5	-5	O
5.	-5	5	-5	O
6.	-5	5	-5	O
7.	-5	O	5	O
8.	5	5	-5	O
9.	-5	O	5	O
10.	-5	-5	5	O
11.	-5	5	-5	O
12.	5	-10	O	O
13.	5	-5	5	O
14.	-5	5	5	O
15.	5	5	-5	O
16.	5	-5	O	O
17.	5	5	-5	O
18.	5	-5	10	O
19.	5	5	-5	O
20.	-10	5	5	O
21.	-5	5	5	O
22.	-10	-5	5	O
23.	-5	5	5	O
24.	-5	O	5	O

TOTAL _____

ULTIMATE 65 TO 125
COMPETENT 0 TO 60
INCONSISTENT -5 TO -70
CLUELESS -75 TO -140

CHAPTER EIGHT: HELPFUL HINTS OR ATTACKS?

	A	B	C	D
1.	5	-5	5	O
2.	5	O	-5	O
3.	-5	5	5	O
4.	-5	-5	5	O
5.	-5	10	O	O
6.	5	-5	5	O
7.	5	-10	-5	O
8.	-5	5	5	O
9.	-5	5	10	O
10.	5	-5	10	O
11.	5	-5	5	O
12.	5	-5	5	O
13.	5	-5	-5	O
14.	-5	-5	5	O
15.	-5	5	5	O
16.	-5	5	5	O
17.	-5	-5	5	O
18.	-5	5	5	O
19.	-5	O	10	O
20.	-5	5	5	O

TOTAL _____

ULTIMATE 60 TO 120
COMPETENT 0 TO 55
INCONSISTENT -5 TO -105
CLUELESS -60 TO -105

CHAPTER NINE: COMMUNICATION

	A	B	C	D
1.	-5	-5	5	O
2.	-5	5	-5	O
3.	-5	-5	5	O
4.	-10	-5	5	O
5.	-5	-5	5	O
6.	-5	-5	5	O
7.	-5	5	5	O
8.	-5	5	-5	O
9.	5	-10	-5	O
10.	5	-5	-5	O

TOTAL _____

ULTIMATE 30 TO 50
COMPETENT 0 TO 25
INCONSISTENT -5 TO -30
CLUELESS -35 TO -60